The Cancer Book
Everything You Should Know About Cancers

CRAFTED BY SKRIUWER

Copyright © 2025 by Skriuwer.

All rights reserved. No part of this book may be used or reproduced in any form whatsoever without written permission except in the case of brief quotations in critical articles or reviews.

At **Skriuwer**, we're more than just a team—we're a global community of people who love books. In Frisian, "Skriuwer" means "writer," and that's at the heart of what we do: creating and sharing books with readers worldwide. Wherever you are in the world, **Skriuwer** is here to inspire learning.

Frisian is one of the oldest languages in Europe, closely related to English and Dutch, and is spoken by about **500,000 people** in the province of **Friesland** (Fryslân), located in the northern Netherlands. It's the second official language of the Netherlands, but like many minority languages, Frisian faces the challenge of survival in a modern, globalized world.

We're using the money we earn to promote the Frisian language.

For more information, contact : **kontakt@skriuwer.com** (www.skriuwer.com)

TABLE OF CONTENTS

CHAPTER 1: INTRODUCTION TO THE CANCER SIGN

- *Origins of Cancer in astrology*
- *The crab symbol and early myths*
- *Water sign and cardinal quality*

CHAPTER 2: TYPICAL TRAITS AND BEHAVIORS

- *Strong feelings and empathy*
- *Protective nature and need for security*
- *Dealing with shifting moods*

CHAPTER 3: THE EMOTIONAL SIDE OF CANCER

- *Recognizing and handling deep emotions*
- *Ways to cope with sadness and anger*
- *Finding healthy emotional outlets*

CHAPTER 4: HOME AND FAMILY FOCUS

- *Creating a nurturing and welcoming space*
- *Roles within the family and traditions*
- *Balancing work duties and home life*

CHAPTER 5: FRIENDSHIP AND LOVE

- *Building trust in relationships*
- *Romantic loyalty and emotional closeness*
- *Overcoming fears of rejection*

CHAPTER 6: CAREER AND GOALS

- *Cancer's approach to work and ambition*
- *Finding stability and security in jobs*
- *Handling stress and office dynamics*

CHAPTER 7: CREATIVITY AND HOBBIES

- *Expressing feelings through art*
- *Enjoyable pastimes for relaxation*
- *Turning hobbies into personal growth*

CHAPTER 8: DAILY ROUTINES AND HABITS

- *Structured vs. flexible routines*
- *Self-care in everyday life*
- *Maintaining emotional balance*

CHAPTER 9: COMMUNICATION STYLES

- *Gentle talk and attentive listening*
- *Conflict resolution strategies*
- *Avoiding silent resentments*

CHAPTER 10: CHALLENGES AND WEAKNESSES

- *Over-sensitivity and mood swings*
- *Fear of conflict and letting go*
- *Handling guilt and anxiety*

CHAPTER 11: STRENGTHS AND POTENTIAL

- *Empathy as a powerful asset*
- *Emotional intelligence in action*
- *Loyalty, resilience, and creative vision*

CHAPTER 12: HANDLING EMOTIONAL UPS AND DOWNS

- *Identifying triggers for mood shifts*
- *Techniques to manage stress or sadness*
- *Importance of sharing feelings safely*

CHAPTER 13: RELAXATION AND SELF-CARE

- *Gentle daily routines for calm*
- *Self-compassion vs. self-criticism*
- *Balancing alone time and social needs*

CHAPTER 14: SPIRITUAL AND MYSTICAL THOUGHTS

- *Connection to the Moon and natural cycles*
- *Rituals, symbols, and intuitive practices*
- *Finding deeper meaning in daily life*

CHAPTER 15: BONDS WITH OTHER ZODIAC SIGNS

- *Compatibility highlights and friction points*
- *Tips to build harmony in friendships or love*
- *Learning from each sign's perspective*

CHAPTER 16: CULTURAL STORIES AND LEGENDS

- Myths of the crab constellation
- Ancient traditions and modern lore
- Lessons and symbolism for Cancer

CHAPTER 17: HEALTH TIPS

- Managing stress and emotional well-being
- Nutrition, exercise, and mind-body care
- Balancing empathy with physical self-care

CHAPTER 18: SUPPORT FOR PERSONAL GOALS

- Defining meaningful aims
- Overcoming self-doubt
- Combining personal ambition with family needs

CHAPTER 19: NOTABLE CANCER FIGURES

- Artists, leaders, and social activists
- Life lessons from real examples
- Inspiration for modern Cancers

CHAPTER 20: FINAL THOUGHTS AND CLOSURE

- Recap of major themes and insights
- Balancing self-care with empathy
- Embracing the path ahead with confidence

CHAPTER 1: AN INTRODUCTION TO THE CANCER SIGN

Astrology is a system that groups dates and times of the year under different names. These names are the zodiac signs. Each sign has special features and interests. One of these signs is Cancer. When we talk about the Cancer sign, we do not mean the sickness. We mean the star sign named "Cancer." If your birthday is between June 21 and July 22, you are usually called a Cancer. In this chapter, we will look at what Cancer means in astrology. We will see why it is called Cancer, which element it belongs to, and how people have thought about it over the years.

What Is Astrology?

Astrology is an old system that tries to connect the positions of the Sun, Moon, and planets with our personalities. It also links these positions to how we act or feel. Long ago, people watched the sky and saw patterns in the stars. They divided the sky into different sections, and each section was called a sign. Over many centuries, people wrote down how they felt these signs might shape thoughts, feelings, and actions.

The zodiac is a group of twelve signs. Each sign covers a part of the year. Cancer is the fourth sign in this group. Some people think astrology is fun, and they like to read about it. Others see it as a way to learn about themselves and other people. There are also many who do not believe in it at all and think it is just a story. However, many still like to talk about astrology and wonder if the descriptions match their lives.

Astrology tries to explain how a sign can shape the way someone sees the world. Each sign is linked to an element (fire, earth, air, or water) and a quality (cardinal, fixed, or mutable). These elements and qualities are said to point to certain patterns in thinking, feeling, or acting. Cancer, for example, is connected to the water element and the cardinal quality.

People born under the Cancer sign often read descriptions that say they might be more emotional or caring. But remember, these descriptions are not rules. Each person is unique. Still, many enjoy learning about the sign they were born under and reading about the traits that might match them.

Where Cancer Fits in the Zodiac

The zodiac starts with Aries, then Taurus, Gemini, and Cancer as the first four signs. After Cancer, there are eight more signs: Leo, Virgo, Libra, Scorpio, Sagittarius, Capricorn, Aquarius, and Pisces. Each sign has a part of the year. Cancer is usually from June 21 to July 22, though some people might place the dates slightly differently, like June 20 to July 21.

Cancer is the only sign linked to a crab. It is often shown as a crab with claws. This sign is also connected to the Moon. The Moon is considered Cancer's ruling planet in astrology. Some say that the Moon's phases might affect the moods or feelings of a Cancer person. In stories about the zodiac, Cancer is seen as caring but also protective, like a crab with a hard shell.

The zodiac signs are often paired with elements. Cancer is one of the water signs. The water signs (Cancer, Scorpio, and Pisces) are said to be more sensitive, intuitive, and thoughtful. The cardinal quality in Cancer means it can take action. Cardinal signs (Aries, Cancer, Libra, and Capricorn) are thought to start new things or lead in certain ways.

Of course, not everyone fits every part of these descriptions. Sometimes, reading about your sign might not match how you feel. Other times, you might see that it matches very well. Astrology is not perfect or scientific, but it is a piece of culture that has existed for a long time.

Why Is It Called "Cancer"?

In Latin, "Cancer" means "crab." This name was chosen by ancient people who named the signs. Each sign has a symbol and a story. The symbol for Cancer looks a bit like two small circles with tails that swirl around each other. Some people say it looks like sideways "69," but it is meant to represent crab claws or the crab itself.

Ancient Greek stories tell of a crab that helped a monster called the Hydra in a big battle. This myth, linked to the hero Hercules, gave Cancer a place in the stars. The crab tried to bite Hercules's foot, but Hercules stomped on it. In thanks for its efforts, the goddess Hera placed the crab in the sky as the constellation Cancer.

These stories are old myths that explain how people once tried to make sense of the night sky. They looked up and saw shapes in the stars, gave them names, and told stories about them. The crab shape might not be very clear to everyone who looks at the sky, but once a story catches on, it stays in our culture.

The Crab Symbol

Crabs have hard shells on the outside and softer bodies on the inside. That hard shell can be like a shield, keeping them safe. This is one reason people say Cancer folks might act protective or careful. They can be warm and kind once they feel safe, but they might also be shy at first.

In nature, crabs often move sideways, which is sometimes seen as unusual. This might be linked to the idea that people under the Cancer sign might not do things in the same way as others. They might find their own path. Some say that, like a crab, a Cancer person might back away from a problem instead of going straight at it. Of course, this is just a description and might not apply to everyone.

The crab is also at home on land or in the water, which can represent a connection to both feelings (water) and the outer world (land). People sometimes say a Cancer person can sense the moods around them but also needs time alone to rest, the same way a crab might hide in its shell.

The Element of Water

Cancer is part of the water signs, along with Scorpio and Pisces. In astrology, water is linked to feelings, imagination, and strong inner worlds. A water sign might be more comfortable dealing with emotional topics or comforting others.

Water can be calm, like a quiet pond, or rough, like a stormy sea. This can be linked to how emotions can feel. Cancer, being a water sign, is sometimes said to have mood swings or shifting feelings, almost like waves. But water also brings life. We all need water to live. In the same way, many believe Cancer can offer support and comfort to others.

Sometimes, water signs are thought to be dreamers. They might like to think about big ideas or show creativity in art, stories, or music. But each sign may do it in a different way. Cancer's way might be linked more closely to family themes or personal memories.

The Cardinal Quality

Astrology also groups signs by how they start, hold, or change energy. Cardinal signs begin new seasons. Aries starts spring, Cancer starts summer, Libra starts fall, and Capricorn starts winter (in the northern half of the world). Because of this, cardinal signs are seen as those who might start new plans or take the first step in a process.

For Cancer, this can mean taking action when it comes to caring for loved ones or beginning family-related events. People often view Cancer as a sign that will step forward in matters of the heart. This does not mean that every Cancer person always takes charge. But it can point to the idea that they may have an urge to take the lead in personal or family situations.

The Moon's Influence

In astrology, each sign is said to have a ruling planet. For Cancer, that planet is actually the Moon. The Moon changes its phase every few days, from new to full and back again. Some people feel the Moon's quick changes affect moods. Since Cancer is linked to the Moon, it may have a tie to changing feelings.

The Moon is also thought to represent comfort, the home, and basic needs. This is why Cancer is often linked to ideas of home life and warmth. The glow of the Moon is gentle compared to the Sun. In many cultures, the Moon is connected to nighttime, dreams, and hidden feelings. Because of that, Cancer might be seen as deep, with an awareness of moods that others might not always see.

The Time of Year (June 21 – July 22)

Cancer covers the start of summer in the northern half of the world. The air might be warmer, and the days are long. Some folks see this time as a period to enjoy bright days, more daylight, and a feeling of comfort. Others might notice that the hot weather can also bring a sense of restlessness.

In the southern half of the world, though, these dates fall in the start of winter. So the sign can also be linked to a colder, quieter time in those places. It depends on where you live.

Still, the common idea is that Cancer sits at a time of change in the seasons, and that can go along with its role as a cardinal sign. The days shift from one type of weather to another, and Cancer is right there at that switch.

Cultural Stories About Cancer

Many myths about Cancer revolve around the crab in Greek tales. But there are also other stories from around the world that connect to crabs or to the time of year associated with Cancer. Some cultures had festivals during the late June and early July time, marking long days or focusing on rest. While these might not directly say "Cancer," they do connect to that part of the year.

In modern times, people with birthdays in late June or early July might share stories about how they connect to the crab symbol. They might like items with crab designs or want to read more about watery or moon themes. For some, this is just for fun. For others, it can hold deeper personal meaning.

First Impressions of Cancer

When first meeting a person who calls themselves a Cancer, you might notice certain qualities like a calm voice or a gentle smile. Some might seem a bit shy at first, like they are peeking out from a shell. Others might come across as thoughtful. Of course, this is not always the case. Some Cancers might be loud or outgoing. The star sign alone does not decide someone's personality.

Still, many who like astrology will say that Cancer has a special link to feelings, family, and protection. This is just an introduction. Later chapters will go into the traits and behaviors in more detail, including how Cancer folks might act in friendships, relationships, or at work. Each person is different, but these broad ideas can be fun or helpful to think about.

CHAPTER 2: TYPICAL TRAITS AND BEHAVIORS

Cancer is often described with certain traits. Some are based on the water element, which suggests feelings and a kind heart. Others come from the cardinal quality, which can mean action. Also, the Moon's influence can point to changes in mood or strong emotional depth. In this chapter, we will look at the typical traits people often link with the Cancer sign. We will also see how these traits might show up in day-to-day life, like at home or with friends.

It is important to remember that each person is unique. Not every Cancer will have all these traits. Sometimes people may share only a few of them. Sometimes, other parts of a person's birth chart (like the rising sign or Moon sign) could also affect how they act. Still, we can learn a lot by looking at the general ideas that have been passed down through astrology traditions.

Strong Feelings

Many say that Cancer has powerful feelings. This can mean caring for others deeply. A Cancer person might be quick to feel happy or sad based on what is happening around them. If a friend is upset, a Cancer might feel upset too. If a friend is happy, a Cancer might feel that joy right away.

Some might call this empathy, which is the ability to sense what others feel. Because of this, many people view Cancer as a sign that wants to help or comfort others. This can be a good trait since it can make them kind listeners or supportive friends. However, it can also be challenging if they take on too many emotions from others.

Protective Instinct

Think of a crab protecting itself with its shell. That is often how Cancer's protective side is explained. They might protect not just themselves, but also the people they care about. If someone they love is being hurt or treated badly, they might step in or speak up.

This protective nature can lead them to be good guardians or friends who stand by loved ones. At the same time, it might also mean they worry too much. Some Cancers might feel a need to keep everyone safe, even in small matters.

Need for Security

Cancer is sometimes seen as a sign that wants safety and security. This can mean they like a stable home life. They might prefer a space of their own that feels comfortable. They may like certain objects or routines that help them feel grounded.

Some might describe a Cancer person as someone who looks for a sense of belonging. They might invest time in their family or close circle of friends. Feeling safe is very important. If they sense any threat to their sense of security, they might pull back or act defensively.

Shifts in Mood

Because Cancer is linked to the Moon, which changes shape and phase often, many say that Cancer can have shifts in mood. This does not mean that every Cancer has wild ups and downs. But they can be sensitive. If something happens that makes them feel sad, it might affect them more than it would affect others. On the bright side, they can also feel excitement or love with strong intensity.

For some Cancers, these mood changes might come on quickly. Others might keep their feelings inside until they can no longer hold them in. It is often helpful for a Cancer person to find healthy ways to share or release these feelings, such as talking with a trusted friend or writing in a journal.

Kindness and Compassion

A common trait linked to Cancer is a soft heart. Many say that Cancer has a natural wish to care for others. This can show up in simple ways, like making soup for a sick friend, or in bigger ways, like volunteering to help people in need.

Because Cancer is a water sign, it is said to have a deep inner world where feelings and thoughts can grow. This can lead to creative expression. Some might draw, paint, sing, or write as a way to show their kind hearts. This sense of caring can make them good at comforting someone who is upset.

Sense of Responsibility

Many times, people born under Cancer are said to be responsible. This does not mean they never make mistakes. But they can often worry about duties and tasks. They might feel guilt if they cannot take care of something important.

Their sense of responsibility might tie back to their protective instincts. They want to look after people and handle tasks that ensure everyone is safe or comfortable. When they are at work or at school, they might do their best to meet deadlines and do a good job. They can take things personally if they feel they have failed someone.

Connection to the Past

Cancer is often thought to be connected to memories and the past. Some say they hold onto objects or photos that remind them of happy times. They might like traditions, old stories, or family histories. This can make them great keepers of memories.

However, holding onto the past can sometimes be a problem if it causes them to stay stuck in old patterns or regrets. A Cancer person might replay past events in their mind more than other signs. They might need support in letting go of sad memories so they can move forward with more ease.

Gentle Personality

Though there are always exceptions, many Cancers are described as gentle people who do not enjoy rough conflicts. They might avoid fights or arguments. If they must face a problem, they could choose a softer approach, hoping to talk things through calmly.

Sometimes, others might see this gentleness as a weakness, but it can also be a strength. A gentle nature can help calm tense situations. It can also make it easier for people to trust them or feel safe around them.

Private Nature

A lot of Cancers do not like to share every detail of their lives. They might have a small group of trusted people and keep everyone else at a distance. This could be compared to the crab hiding in its shell.

Being private can mean they need time to warm up to new people. They might not want to open up about personal matters right away. But once they feel comfortable, they can show their caring and friendly side.

Possible Downsides

While these traits can be good, there are also some challenges. Because Cancers can be so caring, they might forget to care for themselves. They might put others first all the time. This can lead to stress or exhaustion.

Also, their private and protective side can make them seem distant or closed off. If they feel hurt or betrayed, they might pull back into their shell and stay quiet, not telling anyone how they feel. This can make problems worse because others might not know what is wrong.

Shifts in mood can also be hard for those around them, who may not understand why a Cancer person feels a certain way. Since they pick up on emotions easily, they can become overwhelmed if there is a lot of tension around them.

Everyday Examples of Cancer Traits

At School: A Cancer child might be the one who comforts a friend who is sad. They might enjoy group projects where they can help everyone work together. But they might also have moments where they want to work alone if they feel shy or worried.

At Work: A Cancer adult might be the person who remembers everyone's birthdays or tries to make sure the office is tidy and welcoming. They might bring snacks to share. If someone is stressed, they might offer a listening ear. But they could also have days when they seem distant, preferring to stay at their desk.

With Friends: A Cancer friend might check on you to see if you need anything, like a ride somewhere or help with a problem. They might notice your feelings even if you have not said anything. They may also worry if they sense you are unhappy but not sharing why.

At Home: Many Cancers like to create a cozy living space. They might pick soft blankets, warm lighting, or comforting colors. They may treasure old family photos or items that hold memories.

Differences Among Cancers

No two people are alike, even if they share the same sign. Some Cancers might be more outgoing, while others are quiet. Some might show their caring side with lots of hugs and words of support, while others do it in a more subtle way.

Factors like life experiences and other astrology placements (like where the planets were when they were born) can shift how these traits show up. For example, a Cancer with a strong influence from a fire sign might be more energetic or outspoken. A Cancer with an air sign influence might be a bit more talkative and logical.

Still, a thread that often ties Cancers together is the idea of caring, sensitivity, and a wish for a comfortable environment.

Misunderstandings

Sometimes, people might misunderstand a Cancer's quiet nature and think they do not want friends. But often, they just need time or a safe space. Others might think a Cancer person worries too much. But that worry often comes from a place of caring.

Another misunderstanding is that Cancers are always sad or moody. In reality, they can be very joyful and funny when they feel comfortable. They can also share lots of laughter with close friends. Their moodiness might just be a response to stress or strong feelings.

Unique Strengths

Deep Understanding: Because Cancers can sense the emotions of others, they can be good at giving advice or simply being there for a friend.

Loyalty: They can be very loyal to friends, family, or partners. They might stand by someone even when times are tough.

Resourcefulness: Like a crab that can handle changing tides, many Cancers can adapt to different situations, especially if it helps their loved ones.

Imagination: Water signs are said to have strong imaginations. Cancer might use that skill in storytelling, art, or other forms of expression.

Handling Their Traits in a Helpful Way

Because these traits can be both helpful and challenging, it is important for a Cancer person to find balance. They might need to learn to step away from drama or too many negative emotions so they do not carry it all on their shoulders. They might also practice ways to share their own feelings without hiding them away.

Talking to friends, writing in a notebook, or even taking some quiet time can help. Even though many Cancers like to be there for others, they should also remember to care for themselves. This way, they can keep their strength and kindness.

How These Traits Show Up in Groups

When a group is planning an event or working on a project, a Cancer might be the one who looks out for how everyone feels. They could be the person who tries to make sure every voice is heard. If someone is left out, they might do what they can to bring that person into the activity.

They might also notice small details. For example, if the room is too cold, they might offer their sweater to a friend. If someone seems worried, they might find a way to cheer them up.

Cancer Traits in Famous People

Though we will talk more about notable Cancer figures in Chapter 19, it can help to look at how these traits appear in the lives of well-known individuals. Many famous Cancers are known for caring about social causes or using their artistic side to connect with fans. Others might keep their private life hidden from the public.

We will save the details for later chapters, but it is clear that some of these traits can appear in people who do big things in the world. They can turn their empathy and creativity into projects, music, or acts of kindness.

Summary of Common Traits

- **Feelings:** Deep, caring, and sensitive

- **Protection:** Standing up for loved ones and themselves

- **Security:** Needing a safe and warm place to relax

- **Mood Changes:** Shifting emotions linked to the Moon

- **Kindness:** A desire to help and comfort

- **Responsibility:** Concern about duties and tasks

- **Memory:** Holding onto the past, both good and bad

- **Gentle Side:** Preferring calm discussions over loud fights

- **Privacy:** Keeping personal matters close

- **Possible Struggles:** Worry, over-caring, mood swings

Overall Look at Cancer Behaviors

Cancers can be loving friends, family members, and partners. They have a natural warmth that others often find comforting. They might take on a caretaker role or try to be the mediator in conflicts. They might have times when they pull back into their own space, but that is usually because they need to handle their own feelings before stepping out again.

When a Cancer person is feeling good, they can be a bright presence. They might share jokes or want to spend time with close friends. When they are feeling down, they may need understanding and support. Because they sense emotions so strongly, it helps if they have a trusted person to talk to or a peaceful place to rest.

CHAPTER 3: THE EMOTIONAL SIDE OF CANCER

When people talk about Cancer in astrology, they often mention feelings. But what does that truly mean? It goes beyond the idea of being "emotional." It means that a person with strong Cancer influences might feel life more deeply than some others. In this chapter, we will look at how those feelings can shape a Cancer person's thoughts, actions, and relationships. We will explore the many sides of their emotional world, how they might handle stress or sadness, and what tools can help them keep a sense of balance.

The Heart at the Center

For many Cancers, their hearts guide them strongly. This is not just about romance, though that can be part of it. It is about being connected to their own feelings and the feelings of others. When a Cancer person walks into a room, they might sense if someone is nervous, upset, or pleased, even if that person tries to hide it. This can be a real gift. It allows them to offer comfort or support at the right time.

However, it also means that Cancers may find it hard to ignore tense situations. If there is disagreement in the family or among friends, they might pick up on the heavy moods. This can be tiring if it happens too often. A Cancer person might need a way to step back and sort out what is theirs to feel and what belongs to other people.

How Emotions Rise and Fall

In many descriptions of Cancer, you will see talk of the Moon's phases. The Moon appears to change shape from new to full and back again over about a month. Some believe that this quick shift can mirror how a Cancer's emotions might rise and fall. One day they may feel cheerful and excited about something new. The next day, they might feel quiet or uneasy.

These changing feelings are not always negative. They can bring bursts of creativity or insight. A Cancer person might have an idea for a song or poem when feelings run high. They might reach out to a friend to share encouragement when they sense that friend is low. The challenge is learning how to handle these shifts without getting lost in them.

Emotional Memory

Memory plays a big role in how a Cancer person experiences emotions. They might remember small details from long ago, like the color of the sky on a special day or the sound of a loved one's laugh. These memories can bring comfort. Remembering good times helps them feel safe and happy.

On the other hand, they might also recall sad or upsetting events with the same clarity. This can make it tough to let go of hurts. If someone said something unkind in the past, a Cancer might carry that memory for a long time. It does not mean they will always hold a grudge, but the feeling linked to the event can linger. Finding healthy ways to release old pain can be an important step for them.

Reading Between the Lines

Because Cancers can sense the emotions of others, they often notice details that might go unseen by others. They might read facial expressions or tones of voice very well. This allows them to show empathy and offer support, sometimes before a friend even asks for help.

But this "emotional radar" can also become overwhelming. If a room is full of tense people, a Cancer might feel tense too, even if nothing is directed at them. They may end up holding onto stress that is not really theirs. Taking quiet moments alone can help them separate their own feelings from the feelings floating around them.

Handling Joy and Excitement

When good things happen, Cancers can light up with strong excitement. They might clap their hands or grin widely, showing childlike happiness. Their enthusiasm can be contagious, spreading to friends and family. They might be quick to share this good mood, perhaps inviting people to spend time together or talk about the happy event.

This warm side can be one of the best gifts a Cancer brings. They can make everyday moments feel special simply by their genuine care. If they taste a sweet dessert they like, they might beam and say it's wonderful. If they watch a movie that touches their heart, they could cry tears of happiness. These expressions come from a real place, and people around them often appreciate it.

Facing Sadness and Disappointment

Cancers feel sadness in a deep way too. They might cry when faced with painful events, or they might need to withdraw and be alone for a time. Some might try to distract themselves by reading or watching shows, but the feelings usually remain close. They can find it hard to move on until they have processed those emotions.

What helps a Cancer face sadness? Often, it can be a gentle talk with someone they trust. Sharing worries out loud can bring relief. Writing can also help them sort out their thoughts, as it gives them a chance to put their feelings into words. Simple acts, like taking a walk in a calm place or enjoying a soft blanket, might also soothe them.

Dealing with Anger

Anger is another emotion that can arise for anyone, including Cancers. Because they do not always like conflict, some Cancers might push anger down or pretend they are not upset. Over time, this hidden anger can turn into resentment or hurt. When it finally surfaces, it might come out in tears or strong words.

Learning healthy ways to handle anger can be very important. This might include talking things over before emotions get too big. It could also mean writing a letter (not necessarily to send, but just to express the feelings), or finding a physical activity that lets out tension. If a Cancer person can speak about the problem early on, they might save themselves from deeper pain later.

Emotional Triggers and Boundaries

An emotional trigger is anything that causes a strong reaction. For Cancers, these triggers might be linked to family, past memories, or a sense of being left out. When these triggers pop up, they can feel upset or defensive quickly.

Setting boundaries can help. A boundary is a limit that protects someone from harm or stress. For example, a Cancer might limit the time they spend with people who bring up painful memories. They might decide not to talk about certain topics that cause too much emotional strain. By knowing their limits, they can take better care of their emotional well-being.

The Role of Imagination

Cancers often have vivid inner worlds. They might daydream about "what if" scenarios. This imagination can be wonderful for writing stories, inventing art, or coming up with new ideas in school or at work. It can also be a place where they rehearse emotional situations before they happen. For example, a Cancer person might imagine a future talk with a friend and plan what they want to say.

However, imagination can sometimes lead to worry if they focus on scary possibilities. They might picture worst-case outcomes or fear that something bad will happen. Recognizing when their imagination is leaning toward worry can help them refocus on reality. Simple grounding exercises, like naming objects in the room or focusing on the present moment, might help calm an overactive mind.

Emotional Overload

Because they take in so many feelings, Cancers may become overwhelmed. This can show up as tiredness, irritation, or a wish to hide away for a while. They might feel drained after spending time in a crowded or tense place. If they do not take breaks, they could become short-tempered or sad without knowing why.

Building small breaks into their schedule can be a big help. Stepping outside to look at the sky, taking a few deep breaths, or sitting quietly in a peaceful room can give them time to let go of extra tension. Overload can happen to anyone, but it can hit a Cancer hard if they do not watch out for signs that they need rest.

Sharing Feelings with Others

Cancers might not always share what is going on inside right away. They could worry about being judged or burdening others. At the same time, they often feel relief once they do open up. Finding someone who listens without making them feel silly or wrong is key.

Trusted friends or family members can provide a safe space. A counselor or therapist can also help by offering professional guidance. Some Cancers find support groups useful if they are dealing with a specific issue. Talking about feelings can be scary at first, but many Cancers discover that it strengthens their bonds with loved ones.

Building Emotional Support Systems

A strong support system means having people or activities that help a Cancer cope with life's ups and downs. This might include close relatives, caring friends, or even pets that offer comfort. It can also involve hobbies, like painting, playing music, or gardening (growing plants). Through these activities, a Cancer person can express themselves without needing to speak.

Learning to recognize who or what makes them feel better is part of self-awareness. Maybe they have an aunt who always knows what to say. Or perhaps going for a run in the park clears their head. By keeping track of these sources of calm, they can return to them when they feel worried or sad.

Coping with Stress and Anxiety

Stress is a normal part of life, but for someone with Cancer traits, it can affect them deeply. They might worry about people they care about or blame themselves if things go wrong. Over time, this can lead to anxiety or trouble sleeping.

Some ways to handle stress include:

- **Physical Activity**: Gentle exercise, like walking or yoga, can help release tension.

- **Creative Outlets**: Drawing, writing, singing, or other forms of art can give emotions a place to go.

- **Relaxation Techniques**: Simple breathing exercises can calm a racing mind. For example, breathing in for four counts, holding for four, and breathing out for four.

- **Talking It Out**: Sharing concerns with a friend can make problems seem smaller.

Understanding Empathy vs. Sympathy

Cancer people often offer empathy rather than just sympathy. Empathy means feeling with someone, trying to step into their shoes. Sympathy is feeling sorry for someone from a distance. Because of Cancer's strong emotional awareness, they can sense the pain or joy of others in a very personal way.

This can be helpful because friends or loved ones feel truly understood. However, it can be draining if the Cancer person feels too much for too many people at once. Learning when to step back, even if only for a short time, is crucial to avoid emotional burnout.

Dealing with Guilt and Shame

Cancers might take on guilt even when they are not to blame. Their caring nature can make them feel responsible for other people's problems. For example, if a family member is upset, a Cancer might think, "Could I have prevented this?" or "Did I do something wrong?" This sense of guilt can grow if not addressed.

Shame is a related feeling. Shame is the sense that "I am bad," rather than "I did something bad." A Cancer person might be hard on themselves if they think they failed someone. They might hide how they feel, worried that others will judge them. Reminding themselves that making mistakes does not define their worth can help. Talking with a trusted friend or a professional can also ease these heavy feelings.

Balancing Kindness with Self-Care

Cancers often want to help others. But too much giving can exhaust them. Imagine a cup of water. If you keep pouring water out without refilling the cup, it will become empty. The same is true for emotional energy.

Learning to say "no" when overwhelmed is an important skill. A Cancer person might feel bad turning someone down, but saying "no" can be the right choice if it means protecting their own well-being. By taking care of themselves first, they can offer better help in the long run.

Handling Emotional Conflict

When arguments happen, Cancer might either pull back or try to smooth things over quickly. They may dislike tension and seek to restore calm. But sometimes, important issues need direct discussion. Avoiding conflict for too long can cause more confusion.

If they find themselves in a heated argument, taking a brief pause to breathe can help. They can say something like, "I need a moment to think before I respond." This small step can stop them from saying something hurtful in the heat of emotion. Later, they can talk about how they feel and what they need, helping to clear the air in a peaceful way.

Emotional Growth Through Reflection

Though we must be careful with certain words, it is fair to say that Cancers often change and develop by looking back on their experiences. They might learn from past joys and pains. Reflection can be done by:

- Writing in a private notebook

- Speaking with a mentor or friend

- Doing an activity that allows quiet thought, like painting or baking

This process of looking at old feelings and events can help them notice patterns. Perhaps they see that each time they ignore their stress, they get headaches or trouble sleeping. By spotting these links, they can make better choices in the future.

Letting Go of Emotional Baggage

Letting go is not easy for a sign that has deep connections to memory. Cancers might worry that by letting go of a painful memory, they are betraying themselves or someone else. In reality, letting go simply means deciding not to carry the pain anymore. They can still keep the lessons learned without holding onto the hurt.

Techniques to let go could include:

- Writing a letter to the past situation and then throwing the letter away

- Practicing mindfulness, focusing on the present moment instead of replaying old events

- Replacing negative thoughts with gentle statements, such as "I am allowed to move forward."

Finding Positive Outlets

A key part of handling the emotional side of Cancer is finding fun or uplifting outlets for their strong feelings. This can be many things:

- **Music**: Listening to songs that match their mood or writing their own tunes

- **Art**: Painting or sketching their feelings, even if no one else sees the result

- **Reading**: Getting lost in a story that helps them understand different viewpoints

- **Outdoor Time**: Spending time near water, if possible, since it can soothe their water-linked sign

These outlets let them release both happy and sad emotions, leaving them feeling lighter.

How Emotions Affect the Body

Sometimes, when a Cancer person feels upset, they might notice a stomach ache, headache, or muscle tension. Emotions can affect the body in real ways. If they hold onto worries or anger, their bodies might show signs of stress. Learning to listen to these signals can help them address emotional issues before they grow too large.

Some might find relaxation exercises help, such as lying flat on the floor and slowly tensing and releasing muscles, starting with the toes and moving up to the forehead. Paying attention to each part of the body can bring calm and remind the Cancer person to breathe deeply.

Trusting Their Own Emotions

Because they are so sensitive, Cancers might doubt their emotional reactions. They may ask themselves, "Am I feeling too strongly?" or "Should I pretend I am not upset?" It is important for them to learn that their emotions are valid signals, like a traffic light telling them when to stop or go.

Of course, they also need to check if their reactions match the situation. If they are experiencing strong anger over a small problem, they might want to explore why that is. Maybe it reminds them of a bigger hurt from the past. By understanding the root cause, they can deal with emotions more calmly.

Expressing Affection and Love

Another part of Cancer's emotional side is how they show love. This can happen in many forms. Some Cancers use words, like telling friends how much they appreciate them. Others cook or bake for their loved ones, seeing that as a way to show care. Small acts of kindness, like picking up a friend's favorite snack, can also be a sign of affection.

They often value loyalty in return. If they feel that someone they love is drifting away, they might become anxious. They may need clear communication to ensure that the bonds they cherish are still strong. Through open conversations and small gestures of warmth, they can keep these connections steady.

Emotions in Group Settings

In a group, a Cancer might become the quiet observer, noting each person's mood. They might sense who feels left out or who is irritated. This can make them good at creating harmony. However, in large groups with loud personalities, a Cancer can feel overshadowed or overwhelmed.

Making sure they have an exit plan can help. This might involve stepping outside for a breather or hanging out in a smaller circle for part of the event. They should not feel guilty for taking a moment to themselves if the environment is too noisy or stressful.

Teaching Others About Emotional Awareness

Sometimes, the Cancer way of being can teach friends and family to pay attention to emotions. By showing kindness, a Cancer might encourage someone else to be gentle too. By being honest about their own feelings, they might give others permission to do the same. In this sense, a Cancer can quietly guide the people around them toward a more caring style of communication.

Facing Emotional Challenges with Courage

While Cancers might seem shy or reserved, they can be quite strong when life becomes difficult. Their love for others can push them to stand up against problems they would normally avoid. They may be fueled by the desire to protect or help the people they hold dear. This courage can feel different from loud bravery. It is a steady determination that comes from the heart.

Important Reminders for the Emotional Side of Cancer

- **Feelings Are Normal**: Being emotional is not a flaw; it is a way of experiencing life deeply.

- **Boundaries Help**: Know when to step back from people or situations that exhaust you.

- **Sharing Is Healing**: If you keep everything inside, it can grow heavier. Talk it out or write it out.

- **Kindness to Yourself**: Show yourself the same care you offer to others.

- **Memories Can Be Tools**: Learn from the past but do not let it trap you.

Moving Toward Better Emotional Health

A Cancer person can work on their emotional health by checking in with themselves daily. Asking simple questions like, "How am I feeling right now?" or "Is there any worry on my mind that I can solve or let go of?" can keep them aware of their inner state. Short rituals, such as lighting a soothing candle or listening to calming music, can also serve as gentle ways to honor their feelings.

They might also explore meditation apps or gentle stretching routines. These can help slow the mind and let the day's worries drift away. Even a few minutes of quiet reflection can make a difference in how they handle the rest of the day.

CHAPTER 4: HOME AND FAMILY FOCUS

For many people influenced by Cancer, home is more than just a place to sleep. It can be a source of comfort, a place to feel safe, and a center of personal identity. They might pour energy into making sure their living space is warm and welcoming. Family, whether it's the family they were born into or the one they form over time, often plays a huge role in their life. In this chapter, we will explore how Cancer people see home, how they handle family ties, and how these themes shape their day-to-day world.

Why Home Matters So Much

Cancer is often called the sign of home and family. This comes from its connection to the crab, which carries its house on its back. The idea is that a Cancer person wants to feel like they have a safe shell. This shell can be a physical house or a mental space of security.

They might carefully arrange furniture to make rooms cozy or fill shelves with items that hold sentimental meaning. Photos, family heirlooms, or small mementos can be seen everywhere. Even if someone with Cancer traits lives in a tiny apartment, they often put personal touches on it to make it feel like their own corner of the world.

Creating a Welcoming Space

A Cancer might enjoy decorating with soft colors, plush blankets, or comfortable seating. They want a place where people can relax. In fact, they might invite friends over for quiet evenings at home rather than going out to loud, crowded spots. A Cancer might also keep favorite snacks or drinks on hand for guests.

This focus on comfort can extend to scent as well. Some Cancers love gentle fragrances, like vanilla or lavender. Candles, diffusers, or fresh flowers might be part of their decor. All of these choices aim to create a soothing environment where both the Cancer person and their visitors feel at ease.

Family Ties and Traditions

Family is often at the heart of a Cancer's life. This does not mean every Cancer has a perfect family or gets along with everyone. It does mean that family relationships can weigh heavily on their mind. They might think about how they can help a sibling or worry about a parent's health.

They also might hold onto traditions. For example, they could enjoy passing down recipes from grandparents or following certain yearly customs with relatives. If a Cancer starts their own family, they may introduce new traditions that keep everyone connected. If they do not have a close biological family, they often form a "chosen family" of friends who fill that role.

Roles Within the Family

Cancer might take on a nurturing role at home. Even if they are not the official caregiver, they could be the person others call when they need advice. They might be the one who remembers birthdays or organizes small gatherings for loved ones. In some cases, they can become the "family historian," keeping track of old photos or stories.

However, taking on so many responsibilities can become a burden. If a Cancer person feels that their family relies on them for everything, they might become stressed or overwhelmed. It is important for them to learn how to share tasks and ask for help when needed.

Emotional Bonds with Loved Ones

Cancer folks often form deep emotional bonds. This can be with parents, siblings, children, or close friends who feel like family. They might sense changes in a loved one's mood before anyone else. They can be quick to offer support, such as a hug, a listening ear, or a warm meal.

But these bonds can also mean that if a family member says something hurtful, it cuts deep. A Cancer might dwell on harsh words or disagreements for a long time. Learning to talk openly about hurts can help them keep the family bond strong without storing resentment.

Conflict at Home

Like any family, tension can arise. When arguments happen, a Cancer might try to keep the peace. They could try to soothe both sides or bring everyone together to talk calmly. Yet they might also take it personally if the conflict disrupts the harmony of their home.

If a quarrel becomes too heated, a Cancer may retreat to a private spot, like their bedroom, to regroup. This is not a sign they do not care. It might be their way of stopping an emotional overload. Later, they might return with a cooler head to see if they can help fix the situation.

Guarding the Home

The concept of a crab with a shell suggests that Cancers can be protective of their home. They might feel uneasy if strangers come into their space without warning. They may lock doors carefully or keep watch over valuables. This does not mean they are paranoid; they simply want to ensure that their safe place remains secure.

When they choose to share their home, it is often an act of trust. Inviting someone inside can feel like opening a piece of their soul. If that trust is broken, a Cancer might find it hard to invite that person over again. They place high value on feeling safe and respected in the home.

Balancing Work and Family

A Cancer person can sometimes get stuck between duties at work and the desire to be with family. They might feel torn if they have a demanding job but also want to spend time caring for a loved one. This can lead to guilt if they cannot be everywhere at once.

Finding a balance might involve setting boundaries with work, like not checking emails late into the night. It could also mean asking family members for understanding during busy times. Clear communication can help them avoid feeling like they are letting anyone down. Over time, they can learn how to split energy between professional goals and home life in a healthy way.

Living Alone as a Cancer

Not all Cancers have big families or many roommates. Some live alone, either by choice or by chance. Even then, the idea of home is important. They might design their space to reflect their inner world. Soft lighting, personal artwork, and favorite books might fill the rooms.

While living alone, a Cancer could still be in close contact with family or friends through calls or messages. They might check in regularly or welcome visitors for cozy gatherings. If they find themselves lonely, they can consider adopting a pet. Many Cancers enjoy caring for animals, who offer companionship in a peaceful setting.

Setting Up a Comfortable Household

If a Cancer has the chance to set up a home from scratch, they might pick furniture that is more about comfort than appearance. Big couches, fluffy pillows, and thick rugs can create a snug atmosphere. They might also have a kitchen stocked with ingredients for home-cooked meals.

Children's artwork, family pictures, or crafts can appear on walls and shelves. Plants might add life to the corners, hinting at the water sign's gentle nature. Music could often be playing in the background—something soft or calm to keep the mood peaceful. The result is a space where people can let their guard down and feel at home.

Hospitality and Kindness

Cancers are known for showing kindness to visitors. If a friend drops by, they might be offered a drink or snack almost immediately. The Cancer host may ask if the friend is hungry or tired. They could keep a basket of blankets in the living room so everyone can curl up and watch a movie comfortably.

This hospitality can be a lovely quality but might also lead to overextending themselves. If they host too often without a break, they may grow tired or irritable. It is okay for them to say that they need a night off. If their friends are true and caring, they will understand.

Home as an Emotional Retreat

One big reason Cancer values home so much is that it provides a space for emotional release. After a stressful day at work or a difficult time at school, they can come home and breathe. They might turn down the lights, take a warm bath, or sit quietly in a favorite chair. This is where they can feel free to cry, laugh, or simply think without fear of judgment.

They may also keep comfort items around: a soft sweater, a beloved stuffed animal from childhood, or a blanket that belonged to a grandparent. These items have personal meaning that helps them feel grounded and safe. It is not uncommon for a Cancer to keep souvenirs from special moments or gifts from loved ones as part of their décor.

Family Gatherings

Whether it is a small or large group, a Cancer may take the lead in bringing people together. They might plan simple get-togethers or dinners. They often pay attention to the emotional tone of these events, hoping everyone feels included and at ease. If a family member is shy, they might try to involve them in conversation or offer them a quiet spot to relax.

They also tend to remember details about what each person likes or dislikes. For instance, if a cousin is allergic to something, the Cancer host will make sure there are safe food options available. This attentiveness can make guests feel valued.

Challenges with Over-Dependence

Sometimes, a Cancer's strong focus on family can lead to over-dependence. They might rely on family members to solve problems they could handle themselves, or they might feel unable to make big decisions without a relative's input. Alternatively, family members might rely too heavily on the Cancer for support, expecting them to always be available.

Setting boundaries is important. For a healthy dynamic, everyone in the family should respect each other's personal space and independence. A Cancer might gently remind family members that they need time for themselves or that they cannot solve every issue. Though this can be hard at first, it usually leads to healthier, more balanced relationships in the long run.

Different Kinds of Families

Family comes in many forms. Some Cancers are close to grandparents, aunts, uncles, or cousins. Others might have step-parents and half-siblings. Some grow up in foster families or are adopted. Regardless of the structure, a Cancer's desire for a loving and secure environment does not change.

They might build strong bonds with people who are not blood-related but feel like kin. Close friends, godparents, or mentors can become just as important as relatives. Cancers usually focus on loyalty and emotional safety rather than formal labels.

Passing on Values

In many cases, Cancers want to pass on values to the next generation or to loved ones. These values might include kindness, honesty, and respect. They may share stories of their own childhood or how their parents used to do certain things. They might also make sure their children or younger relatives learn manners, empathy, or the importance of caring for others.

This passing on of values can happen through simple daily moments, like showing kids how to comfort someone who is sad or taking them along when helping a neighbor. It might also happen during important times, like big family meals or special occasions. Either way, it shows the Cancer's wish to make sure loved ones grow up in a supportive environment.

The Idea of "Home" Away from Home

A Cancer might feel uneasy when traveling or living somewhere far from familiar surroundings. They might miss their bed, their favorite mug, or the quiet spot on the couch. To help with this, they can bring little touches of home with them: photos of loved ones, a small blanket, or even a special pillow.

If they are moving long-term, they may try to recreate a cozy feel in their new place. Soft lighting, personal decorations, and items that remind them of family can ease homesickness. Even a few minutes of video chatting with a loved one can give them a sense of being closer to home.

Problems That Arise in the Household

No household is perfect. A Cancer might face arguments over chores, spending, or how to handle a family event. Their desire for harmony might lead them to take on more than their fair share. For instance, they might do most of the cleaning or cooking without asking others to pitch in. Over time, this can cause resentment.

Learning to delegate tasks can help. A Cancer can calmly explain that everyone living in the same space should share responsibilities. It might feel awkward at first, but standing up for fairness is important for long-term peace.

Care for Younger Family Members

When children are involved, a Cancer often becomes very protective. They might be the one who attends every school function or coaches a child through tough emotions. They might also place a lot of importance on routines, such as bedtime stories or meal times together. These routines help children feel safe and teach them the value of emotional closeness.

However, it is also possible to be too protective. If a Cancer never allows a child to explore or make mistakes, the child could miss out on learning life lessons. Striking a balance is key—offering a safety net but also letting children grow at their own pace.

CHAPTER 5: FRIENDSHIP AND LOVE

When people think of Cancer's relationships, they often focus on how caring this sign can be. While it is true that Cancers can care deeply, there is much more to their connections with friends and partners. In this chapter, we will look at how Cancer folks form and keep close friendships, what they might search for in love, and the ways they show affection. We will also see how they handle challenges, like disagreements in friendships or trouble in romantic bonds.

Building Friendships with Cancer

A Cancer person might not make friends instantly. They can be a bit guarded at first. But when they decide to let someone in, they tend to give a great deal of kindness. Friends of Cancer often say they feel safe opening up about problems or worries because Cancer listens closely without quick judgment.

Trust and Loyalty

Trust is key for a Cancer. Before they consider someone a real friend, they want to see signs of honesty. If a friend shows they can be trusted with a secret, Cancer will likely open up more. From that point on, loyalty becomes a major theme. Cancers do not like to abandon people they care about. They prefer to work through issues rather than walk away.

Helping Hands

Cancers often help their friends in ways that might seem small but can mean a lot. They might remember a friend's favorite snack and bring it to them when they sense that friend is having a tough day. They could send thoughtful messages just to check in. While some signs might show affection through bold actions, Cancer often uses gentle gestures.

How Cancer Handles Disagreements with Friends

Even in good friendships, disagreements can happen. A Cancer might try to avoid big fights by stepping back and giving the other person time to calm down. However, if they feel strongly about something, they will let the friend know. They prefer to solve problems in a calm setting, maybe sitting together in a quiet room rather than a noisy place.

Because they are sensitive, harsh words can sting. If a friend says something upsetting, a Cancer might hold onto that hurt for longer than expected. Apologies matter a lot to them. If the friend shows real regret, a Cancer is often willing to mend the bond.

The Meaning of Friendship for Cancer

For a Cancer, friendship is often more than casual fun. It is a bond where people share support and time. This does not mean they cannot enjoy silly moments or jokes. They do like laughing with friends. But beneath that, they also hope to find understanding.

They may share personal stories about their families or past. A Cancer might introduce a close friend to their home or favorite cozy spots. This is a sign of trust, showing that the friend is truly valued.

Friend Group Size

Some Cancers have a small circle of close companions. They invest time and care into these connections. Others might have a wider group but still keep a few best friends who know them deeply. In either case, they prefer genuine bonds rather than many shallow ones.

Love and Romance: An Overview

When it comes to love, Cancers often wear their hearts on their sleeves. They can show tenderness early on, though they might also be shy about revealing deeper emotions until they feel safe. In a relationship, they might be quick to show concern for their partner's needs, offering small gifts or kind words.

Emotional Intimacy

Because Cancers feel things strongly, they often look for someone who respects their emotions. They like to know that their worries and joys are taken seriously. If their partner brushes off their feelings as silly, Cancers might withdraw. On the flip side, a supportive partner who listens can form a deep and lasting bond with a Cancer.

Security and Comfort

Security is a common theme for Cancer. They want to feel that their relationship is stable. This does not mean they shy away from excitement. Rather, they enjoy excitement in a setting where both people trust each other. Feeling safe allows them to show their full range of feelings without fear.

Courtship Style

When showing interest in someone, a Cancer might do small, caring acts. They might send a heartfelt note or prepare a home-cooked meal. Some prefer to keep it simple, like giving a book that reminded them of the other person. These actions can mean more to a Cancer than grand displays.

Shyness vs. Openness

Not every Cancer is the same. Some might be quite direct when they like someone. Others can be more reserved, hinting at their interest rather than stating it outright. If the other person seems warm and friendly, they may become more open. If they sense rejection or coldness, they might back away.

Deep Emotional Bonds in Love

Cancers often treat their partners like family. They may want to involve them in family gatherings or share memories from childhood. They see love as an emotional bond, not just a casual connection.

Expression of Feelings

They can show love in many ways: cooking meals, offering warm hugs, writing sweet messages, or simply spending quiet time together. They might place value on shared evenings at home, watching a movie or discussing the day.

If their partner does not return these gestures or seems distant, Cancers can worry. They might start asking, "Is something wrong? Are you upset?" because they sense changes in mood. A good partner for Cancer often understands this caring nature and offers reassurance.

Handling Relationship Challenges

No relationship is perfect. When a problem pops up, a Cancer might become emotional. They could need time to process their feelings before talking about the issue. Some might cry, some might go silent, and others might speak openly.

Conflict Resolution

Cancers prefer calm talks where both people listen. They often say, "Please tell me how you feel." This is their way of seeking understanding. If anger flares on the other side, they could close up or leave the room to avoid a shouting match. Later, they might come back to talk it through once everyone has cooled off.

Fear of Losing the Bond

Because they value stability, Cancers can fear that a disagreement might lead to a breakup. They may hold on tightly or try extra hard to fix things. While this can show devotion, it can also be draining if the partner is not equally invested.

Signs of Love from Cancer

Gentle Care: They might take note of small things that bring the partner joy, like a favorite TV show or treat.

Protectiveness: They can stand up for their partner if someone else is being unfair.

Thoughtful Surprises: These are not always fancy gifts but might be a meaningful letter or handmade item.

Listening Ears: They pay attention to stories about the partner's day, remembering details.

Physical Warmth: Some Cancers enjoy hugs, cuddles, or a simple hand-hold.

How Cancer Deals with Heartbreak

If a breakup happens, it can be very painful for a Cancer. They might need time alone to process sadness. Old memories could replay in their mind, making it hard to let go. Talking with a close friend or spending time at home can help them work through the emotions.

Moving Forward

Eventually, many Cancers try to remember the good times but accept that the relationship ended for a reason. Some keep mementos of past relationships, not to cling to them, but because they value memories in general. When they are ready, they can open their heart to someone new.

Maintaining Friendship After Love Ends

Sometimes, a Cancer can stay friends with a former partner if the parting was peaceful. They might still feel concern for that person's well-being, though they will set boundaries to protect their own heart. If the breakup was harsh, they may cut off contact to avoid further hurt.

Cancer's Ideal Partner Traits

Emotional Awareness: Understanding that feelings matter and giving space for them.

Loyalty: Showing they will stand by the Cancer, especially when times get tough.

Respect for Home Life: Valuing comfort and warmth, possibly sharing an interest in a snug living space.

Patience: Allowing time for the Cancer to open up fully.

Open Communication: Being honest and kind even during disagreements.

Cancers in Long-Term Bonds

When a Cancer finds a stable relationship, they usually give it their all. They might see it as a shared life, not just a casual tie. This can be seen in how they plan for the future, talk about living arrangements, or consider ways to help each other grow in personal goals.

In these bonds, romance might be shown in daily acts. For example, they might make coffee for the partner every morning, or text sweet notes during the day. While they might not always speak about big romantic gestures, their steady kindness can create a sense of closeness.

Challenges in Romantic Relationships

Mood Shifts: Cancers can have changing feelings, causing confusion for a partner who cannot guess the reason.

Overgiving: They might do too much for a partner, leading to imbalance.

Fear of Abandonment: They can worry if the partner seems distant, imagining worst-case scenarios.

Overly Protective: While protection can be sweet, it might feel limiting if the partner needs more personal space.

Learning to Give and Receive in Love

A strong Cancer relationship has give and take. Cancers are often quick to offer help or affection, but they must also learn to receive these things. If they only give, they might end up drained. A healthy partner will notice their needs and return the care.

It can help if the partner expresses thanks for each act of kindness. This shows the Cancer that their efforts are seen. At the same time, Cancer should allow the partner to show their own style of caring. Every person has a different way of showing love.

Friendship vs. Romance: Key Differences for Cancer

Though friendships and romances can look similar for a Cancer—both include caring and closeness—there are differences. In romance, Cancer might share more private thoughts or deeper fears. They might also make plans involving building a life together (or the idea of a shared future).

In friendship, Cancer values loyalty but may not feel the same level of strong emotional attachment as in love. Still, they might treat a best friend almost like a sibling, inviting them to family events or trusting them with personal matters.

Supporting a Cancer Friend or Partner

If you have a Cancer friend or partner, there are helpful things you can do:

- **Listen Patiently**: Let them share their worries or joys.

- **Offer Comfort**: A kind word or a calm environment can mean a lot to them.

- **Be Honest**: They prefer knowing the truth rather than sensing something is off.

- **Respect Their Space**: They might need time alone to sort through feelings.

By doing these things, you show that you understand their nature. This encourages them to stay open and trusting.

Friendship Groups and Social Events

Some Cancers enjoy hosting close gatherings where a few friends meet to talk and relax. Large parties might make them anxious unless they know everyone there. They can be friendly, but they often feel more comfortable in smaller circles.

If a Cancer does go to a big event, they might stick to people they already know. Or they may find a corner to talk with one friend rather than mingle with strangers. This is not because they dislike new people—often it is just how they handle their sensitivity in busy environments.

Romantic Gestures That Appeal to Cancer

- **Home-Cooked Dinners**: A cozy meal at home can make them feel warm and loved.

- **Soft Surprises**: A heartfelt note hidden somewhere for them to find.

- **Calm Outings**: Trips to a quiet beach or a peaceful park, where they can talk without too many distractions.

- **Memory-Keeping**: Making a small photo album or scrapbook of shared moments.

These gestures tap into Cancer's love for comfort, emotion, and personal detail.

Navigating Jealousy

Some Cancers feel jealous if they think their friend or partner is drifting away. This can happen in friendships too, not just romantic ties. They might worry that a close friend is spending more time with someone else.

The best way to handle this is open communication. Asking, "I'm feeling left out. Is there something going on?" can clear the air. If the friend or partner reassures them, most Cancers can relax. If not, they may dwell on thoughts of losing that bond, which can lead to sadness or anger.

Moving from Friendship to Romance

Because trust is so important, some Cancers find romantic partners among their friends. A close friend who already knows their emotional side may be a good fit. If both people feel a spark, the friendship can shift into love.

However, they might worry about ruining the friendship if the romance fails. That risk can make them hesitant. They might hold back until they are sure the feelings are mutual. If they decide to take that step, they often do so with careful thought, aiming to keep the friendship strong even if dating does not go as planned.

Helping a Cancer Through Heartbreak

If you have a Cancer friend who is hurting after a breakup, you can:

- **Be Available**: Let them talk about their feelings.

- **Offer a Comfortable Environment**: Maybe watch a gentle movie together or go for a slow walk.

- **Remind Them of Their Value**: Encourage them to see their good qualities.

- **Give Them Time**: They might need a while to heal, and that is okay.

They can recover, but it may happen step by step rather than quickly.

Building Friendships That Last

One special thing about friendships with Cancer is that they can last for many years. Even if the friends live far apart, Cancer will remember birthdays or important dates. They might send cards or messages out of the blue just to say, "I'm thinking of you."

Over time, these friendships can feel more like a family bond. If the friend is in trouble, Cancer may drive hours to help. In return, they hope the friend would do the same. These kinds of solid friendships can bring real joy to Cancer's life.

Romance Over the Years

In long-term romantic relationships, Cancer's caring spirit can grow stronger with time. They may become more comfortable expressing needs, fears, and dreams. They might also encourage their partner to share more, creating a safe atmosphere for both people.

Sometimes, habits form, like a nightly routine of chatting about the day. These little rituals can help keep the connection strong. If the relationship hits a bumpy phase, the couple can rely on their history of emotional honesty to guide them.

Setting Boundaries in Relationships

While they are often giving, Cancers also need to set boundaries so they do not lose themselves in a friendship or romance. For example, if a friend constantly asks for favors but never returns them, Cancer might learn to say, "I can't help this time."

In love, if the partner expects Cancer to handle all emotional or household tasks, Cancer might gently explain that they need shared effort. Setting these limits is important to avoid burnout.

Dealing with Nontraditional Relationships

Not everyone follows the same relationship path. Some prefer open relationships, some prefer living alone, and so on. A Cancer might be cautious with nontraditional setups because they value security. However, each Cancer is different. Some may find ways to feel safe in unique relationship styles.

They will likely talk things out in detail, making sure everyone's emotions are respected. If they can reach an arrangement that feels stable, they might adjust. If they cannot find emotional safety, they may decide that the setup is not for them.

Friendship and Love Across Distances

In our world, many people have friends or partners who live far away. A Cancer might keep these connections strong through frequent calls, messages, and shared photos. They might send care packages or postcards to remind the person that they are still in each other's thoughts.

They could worry about drifting apart, so they try to keep contact active. This can be a great help, but they also need to remember that life can get busy. If a friend or partner does not reply at once, it may not mean the bond is fading. Learning to trust is key.

Giving and Receiving Gifts

Cancers often enjoy giving gifts that have personal meaning—maybe a handmade scarf or an item that calls back to an inside joke. They love receiving gifts that show thoughtfulness too. For instance, a small token that relates to a memory they shared with a friend can warm their heart more than an expensive but impersonal present.

Shared Activities with Friends or Loved Ones

Activities that let a Cancer connect on a personal level are ideal. They might enjoy:

Cooking Together: Trying a simple recipe in the kitchen.

Watching Movies: Especially stories that have strong emotional themes.

Visiting Quiet Places: Beaches, lakes, or parks where they can talk or sit together.

Creative Projects: Such as painting a picture or writing a short story side by side.

These shared moments help deepen bonds in a calm, comfortable way.

CHAPTER 6: CAREER AND GOALS

For many people under the Cancer sign, work is about more than just earning money. It can be a place to express kindness, create security, and support their home life. In this chapter, we will look at the ways Cancers might approach a career, how they set goals for the future, and what matters most to them in the workplace. We will also see the kinds of jobs that might appeal to their caring side, and how they handle challenges like stress or competition on the job.

The Concept of Work for Cancer

While some signs might chase status or adventure in their jobs, Cancers often seek stability. A typical Cancer might prefer a work environment that feels supportive and friendly. They might be less interested in loud recognition and more focused on doing their tasks well, in a space where they can feel comfortable.

However, comfort does not mean they lack ambition. Many Cancers do have goals, but they often tie those goals to creating a secure life. This might mean saving money for a home or providing for family rather than chasing the highest possible position.

Traits That Can Help in Careers

Cancers bring certain strengths to the workplace:

Empathy: They can sense the needs of clients, coworkers, or customers. This can be an asset in jobs where helping people is key.

Attention to Detail: They might notice small errors or remember instructions well, which can be helpful in many fields.

Loyalty: They often stay in a workplace for a long time if they feel valued, leading to deep experience.

Patience: They can remain calm in certain stressful moments, especially if they have a clear plan.

At the same time, these strengths can backfire if a Cancer takes on too much emotional weight or tries to please everyone at the expense of their own energy.

Balancing Home and Work

Since home is important for Cancer, they often try to balance work with personal life. They might seek jobs that allow flexible schedules or at least let them spend enough time with family. If a job demands too many late nights or constant travel, a Cancer could become unhappy over time.

For them, success is not only about a title; it is also about having a life outside of work. They might turn down promotions if the new role would take them away from loved ones too often.

Possible Career Paths

Cancers can thrive in many fields, but certain areas stand out:

Healthcare: Their caring nature can lead them to roles like nursing, counseling, or therapy.

Teaching: Some Cancers enjoy guiding children or adults, sharing knowledge in a nurturing environment.

Social Work: Again, their empathy helps them connect with those who need assistance.

Hospitality: Running a bed and breakfast, working in hotels, or even cooking in a restaurant can suit their wish to make others feel welcome.

Art or Design: Their sensitivity can fuel creativity. They might enjoy interior decorating, painting, or craft-based work, especially if it allows them to create a warm atmosphere.

Office Roles With a Personal Touch: For example, human resources or roles that involve interacting with and supporting coworkers.

These are not the only options. Some Cancers may excel in business, science, or technology, especially if they see how their work can help people or bring a sense of security.

Leadership Style

If a Cancer takes on a leadership role, they often lead with a caring approach. They might listen to employees' concerns, try to create a pleasant team environment, and offer constructive feedback. They can be protective of their team, standing up for them if upper management is unreasonable.

However, Cancers might struggle with making tough decisions that affect people negatively, such as layoffs or cutting budgets. They can learn to handle these tasks by focusing on fairness and clear communication. If they see that changes are necessary, they will try to soften the impact on those involved.

Workplace Challenges

Cancers can face certain struggles at work:

Taking Criticism Personally: They might feel hurt if a boss or coworker points out a mistake, even if it is done politely.

Emotional Overload: In jobs with heavy emotional demands (like social work), they can absorb others' stress.

Fear of Change: Quick shifts in company policy or job structure can make them uneasy. They prefer to plan and adjust at a calmer pace.

Standing Up for Themselves: If others try to take advantage of their kindness, they might need to learn to set boundaries.

Recognizing these issues can help a Cancer find ways to cope, such as taking short breaks or seeking support from a mentor.

Setting Goals

Cancers usually set goals that link to security. For instance, they might save money to buy a house or to have a cozy nest egg. They might also set goals around helping others, like aiming to open a small daycare or volunteer group. These goals match their nature: caring for people and securing a stable future.

Short-Term vs. Long-Term Goals

- *Short-Term*: Finding a job that is stable, learning new skills that can help them do their tasks better, or earning enough to support immediate home needs.

- *Long-Term:* Building a career that allows them to spend quality time with loved ones, investing in a property that feels like a safe haven, or starting a family-oriented business.

Staying Motivated

To stay motivated, Cancers often remember why they are working. This might be to provide a comfortable home or support their children's education. They might keep pictures of loved ones in their workspace or decorate their desk with items that bring them calm feelings.

If they lose track of their purpose, they can become tired or restless. Regular check-ins with themselves help: "Am I on the right path? Does this job still match my need for security and care?" If not, they might look for a new position that fits them better.

Working with Coworkers

Cancers can be good teammates. They listen to others, share tasks, and avoid pushing themselves forward for praise. However, they need to be careful not to let more forceful coworkers load them with extra work. Since they do not like conflict, they might silently accept tasks without protesting.

If they feel overwhelmed, it helps to practice politely but firmly saying, "I already have my hands full; can we share this task with someone else?" This approach can prevent burnout and teach colleagues to respect boundaries.

Communication Style in the Workplace

Their communication often has a gentle tone. They might prefer face-to-face talks over sending emails about sensitive matters. If a dispute arises, they are more likely to request a private discussion than address it in front of the whole office.

This gentle style can be a plus for building harmony. But it can also mean that direct coworkers or bosses may misunderstand them as passive. Cancers can learn to be clear and assertive while keeping their warm approach.

Handling Workplace Stress

In a high-pressure environment, a Cancer may become anxious. They might worry about letting down the team or losing job security. If they pick up on coworkers' stress, it can add to their own. Here are some ways they might cope:

Finding a Quiet Moment: Taking a short break in a calm area to breathe and refocus.

Talking to a Trusted Colleague: Sharing concerns with someone who can offer empathy.

Keeping Personal Comforts: A photo of family, a favorite snack, or even a comforting item on their desk.

Sticking to Schedules: Having a plan for the day can reduce worry about the unknown.

Career Growth for Cancer

Some Cancers advance by slowly building experience in one place, becoming a pillar of the company. Others might switch jobs if they see a chance for better stability or a friendlier environment. They do not always chase the biggest promotions; they look for roles where they feel useful and supported.

If they do aim for a leadership position, they often excel at building a close-knit team. They might personally train new employees, share tips, and ensure everyone feels included. This sense of unity can lead to strong results.

Self-Employment and Small Businesses

Because Cancers like a cozy atmosphere, some choose self-employment. Running a small store, cafe, or child-care service can let them control the environment, creating a welcoming spot that reflects their warmth. They can decorate as they like and set rules that ensure harmony.

However, self-employment comes with risk. This might worry a Cancer who wants guaranteed stability. They often handle this by planning carefully before launching a business. They might save money ahead of time or do research to ensure that the venture has a solid chance.

Handling Competition

Some work fields are very competitive. Cancers might find this stressful, as they do not enjoy pushing others aside to get ahead. However, if they believe in what they do, they can bring a quieter form of determination. They might show consistent hard work, friendly relationships, and patient progress until they achieve recognition.

In a competitive setting, they can learn to defend their ideas without feeling guilty. Reminding themselves that everyone deserves a fair chance can help them see that standing up for themselves is not wrong. It is just part of a balanced work life.

Financial Goals and Management

Money often ties to security for Cancer. They might keep careful track of what they earn and spend, ensuring they have enough for rent, groceries, and savings. Some like to have an emergency fund so they do not worry about unexpected bills.

They could also look at safe investment options, like real estate or stable funds, rather than taking big risks. This style might not yield huge gains fast, but it aligns with their steady approach to building a strong foundation.

Working in Teams vs. Working Alone

While Cancers can thrive on a team, some do well alone if the job allows them to work at their own pace. For instance, freelance writing, at-home consulting, or online design can suit them if they enjoy peace and quiet. They can then switch to "team mode" for group chats or client meetings.

In a team setting, they often become the go-to person for advice or emotional support. This can make them popular among coworkers, but they should avoid letting that role drain them. It is okay to suggest that a coworker speak to a manager or human resources if the issue is beyond a friendly chat.

Mentoring Others

A Cancer's caring nature can make them excellent mentors. They can guide new hires or younger coworkers, teaching them not just job skills but also how to handle workplace emotions. They might share tips on staying calm under deadlines or approaching conflicts fairly.

Mentoring can give them a sense of purpose. They see someone else grow in confidence or skill. This can be rewarding, though they should remember to keep healthy boundaries. Constantly worrying about a mentee's problems can become overwhelming.

Risk-Taking vs. Caution

In many careers, taking risks can lead to greater rewards. Cancers generally prefer to think things through. They might avoid sudden moves that could harm their sense of stability. Before changing jobs or starting a big project, they usually consider the pros and cons carefully.

If they do take a leap, it is often because they see a long-term benefit, like a better environment or more time for family. Once they commit, they put effort into making it work, leaning on their steady approach and the support of those they trust.

Dealing with Workplace Politics

Office politics can be tricky for Cancer. They usually dislike gossip or backstabbing. If coworkers talk poorly about each other, a Cancer might feel uncomfortable. They might try to stay neutral or quietly leave the conversation.

If they become a target of office politics, they may feel hurt or upset. In such cases, they could speak to a supervisor or look for allies who also value fairness. Being honest about concerns can sometimes ease tensions.

Retirement and Later Goals

When it is time to slow down, many Cancers imagine a peaceful retirement with a comfortable home base. They might think about traveling to see family or spending more time gardening or crafting. If they saved carefully, they can enjoy this stage without constant money worries.

Some Cancers do not fully leave work; instead, they take on part-time roles or volunteer. Their caring side might lead them to help in community centers or local charities. This allows them to keep feeling useful while enjoying a more relaxed pace.

Personal Growth Through Work

Over time, Cancer can grow as a person in the workplace by learning:

- **Assertiveness**: Speaking up about concerns before they become big problems.

- **Self-Care**: Recognizing when they need a break or should delegate tasks.

- **Networking**: Building connections without feeling it is just a cold business move. They can form real friendships, which might lead to job opportunities.

- **Adaptability**: Accepting changes in technology or methods, seeing them as steps forward rather than threats to stability.

These lessons can also help them outside of work, fostering confidence and balance in daily life.

Challenges for Young Cancer Professionals

Younger Cancers entering the workforce might find it daunting. They may worry about fitting in or pleasing a boss. If they face rough personalities, they could doubt themselves. Yet their caring side can be an asset. They might stand out as supportive team members who truly listen.

To succeed, they might seek a mentor, learn to ask questions, and set realistic goals. They can remind themselves that everyone has a learning phase. Over time, they can grow more comfortable voicing ideas and taking on bigger tasks.

Handling Failures or Setbacks

Nobody's career goes perfectly all the time. If a Cancer faces a setback—like losing a job or not getting a promotion—they might take it to heart. They could blame themselves or feel they have let loved ones down.

In these moments, it can help to remember that one setback does not define their worth. They can use a supportive network—family, friends, or mentors—to talk through their feelings and see what lessons can be learned. Afterward, they often come back more determined to find a stable path forward.

Finding Meaning in Work

Because Cancers are guided by emotion and care, they often want to sense that what they do has value. This does not have to be world-changing. Even a small task that helps a neighbor or solves a problem can bring them pride. If a job feels empty or goes against their personal values, they might become restless or sad.

They do not have to work for a charity to find meaning. A Cancer selling products can still feel fulfilled if they believe in those products or enjoy giving customers friendly service. The key is that they see a positive side in their efforts.

Working with Other Zodiac Signs

Though we will talk more about zodiac sign bonds in Chapter 15, a few quick notes about Cancer in teamwork:

With Fire Signs (Aries, Leo, Sagittarius): Cancers might find these signs brash at times, but they can also be inspired by their energy.

With Earth Signs (Taurus, Virgo, Capricorn): Often a good match for practical tasks, though they might differ in emotional expression.

With Air Signs (Gemini, Libra, Aquarius): Communication can be swift, but Cancer may want more depth than they provide.

With Water Signs (Cancer, Scorpio, Pisces): There can be strong understanding, though they risk merging feelings too much if boundaries are not kept.

Planning for Future Goals

To achieve big aims, Cancer can break them down into smaller steps. For example, if they want to open a home-based business, they might:

- Research local rules and permits.
- Save a certain amount of money as a cushion.
- Talk to others who have done something similar.
- Start small to see if there is interest, then expand.

This step-by-step approach helps them avoid feeling overwhelmed and maintains their sense of security.

Supervisors and Mentors for Cancer

When a Cancer finds a good mentor or supportive boss, they can truly shine. They work harder for someone who respects their feelings and acknowledges their strengths. In return, they stay loyal and do their best to help the team.

If they have a harsh boss, they might become anxious or retreat. They might need to speak up or look for a workplace that better suits their style. Over time, they can learn that not every environment will be perfect for them, and that is okay. They can search until they find a better fit.

Succeeding on Their Own Terms

Success for Cancer does not always mean becoming the top person in a company. They might measure success by how comfortable they feel, how well they can provide for loved ones, or how much time they have outside of work. This can lead to more balanced choices than someone who only aims for the highest role.

For instance, a Cancer might pick a mid-level position that offers a pleasant work culture and steady pay over a high-level post with constant stress. They do this because they see the bigger picture: a job that keeps them calm and stable is more important than chasing titles.

CHAPTER 7: CREATIVITY AND HOBBIES

Cancer is often linked with sensitivity and emotional depth. These traits can bring a unique flavor to creative activities and leisure interests. When Cancers explore art, music, writing, or any pastime, their feelings can guide them in special ways. In this chapter, we will look at how Cancer's emotional side influences creativity, the types of hobbies they might enjoy, and how these activities fit into their life. We will also see how they use their free time to relax, grow in skill, and add meaning to their days.

How Feelings Inspire Creativity

Many Cancers are attuned to their own emotions and those of the people around them. This sensitivity can help them create powerful works of art or ideas. For example, if they paint, their art might show gentle or dramatic moods. If they write stories, those stories might include themes of care, family, or strong emotional bonds.

In contrast to someone who simply sees a flower and draws it as it is, a Cancer might draw that same flower with a soft glow or subtle shading that reflects how they feel about it. Their emotions become part of the art, giving it a personal touch.

Artistic Pastimes

Some Cancers gravitate toward visual arts such as painting, sketching, or crafts. They may find that expressing themselves through colors and shapes provides relief from daily worries. Using watercolors can be especially appealing, as the fluid nature of the paint echoes the water element linked to Cancer.

Others might take up sculpture or pottery, enjoying the feeling of shaping something with their hands. This physical aspect can be calming, allowing them to direct their emotional energy into a tactile project. Even if they do not strive to be professional artists, making simple handmade items can bring joy and a sense of achievement.

Music and Song

Music is another area where Cancer's sensitivity can shine. Some might learn to sing or play an instrument, such as the piano, guitar, or violin. The sounds they create can mirror their shifting moods—soft and gentle at times, full of energy at others.

Even if they do not perform publicly, playing music at home can soothe their minds. Listening to certain songs might also help them process feelings. For instance, if they feel down, a comforting melody could help them let the emotion out. If they feel upbeat, a more energetic tune might let them share that enthusiasm.

Creative Writing

Because of their strong inner life, many Cancers enjoy writing. This could be short stories, poetry, personal thoughts, or even writing letters to friends. Their words might carry a sense of warmth and sincerity. They might also be drawn to journaling about daily happenings, dreams, or reflections.

In creative writing, they can channel the emotions they pick up from the world around them. They might explore themes of home, memories, or protecting someone they care about. Writing can also serve as a way to handle stress, allowing them to transfer worries onto the page rather than storing them inside.

Crafts and DIY Projects

Cancers sometimes find peace in doing do-it-yourself (DIY) projects. They might enjoy knitting, sewing, or making handmade gifts for loved ones. These hobbies combine creativity with practicality, which appeals to the part of Cancer that wants to nurture and provide.

Crafts can also help them build a cozy environment, matching their love of home. They might knit blankets or create decorative items that add a personal touch to their living space. If they share these items with friends or family, it becomes another way of showing care, much like cooking a comforting meal.

Connecting Hobbies to the Home

For Cancer, hobbies often revolve around the concept of home and comfort. Some find pleasure in home-related tasks that double as pastimes. For instance, they might enjoy interior decorating, rearranging furniture for a fresh look, or planting herbs in a small kitchen garden.

Others might focus on improving their cooking or baking skills. Trying new recipes can be fun, especially if they can share the results with friends or relatives. The act of cooking itself can be calming, providing structure and a sensory experience—the feel of dough, the sound of chopping, the warmth of the oven.

Outdoor Activities for Cancer

Though Cancers can be homebodies, they also may appreciate gentle outdoor hobbies. Being linked to the water element, many enjoy spending time near lakes, rivers, or the ocean if they have access to these locations. Activities like fishing or relaxing by the shore can soothe their minds.

If they are not near natural waters, they might take walks in a peaceful park, noticing the small changes in seasons or the shapes of leaves. Gardening is another possibility, allowing them to tend to living plants and watch them develop over time. While they might not be fans of extreme sports, calm outdoor activities can nurture their sense of balance.

Group or Solo Hobbies?

Cancers may choose solitary hobbies if they need personal space to think and create. Painting alone or writing in a quiet corner can help them reflect without distraction. If the environment is calm, they can get lost in their imaginations for hours.

However, they might also like group activities that feel friendly and relaxed. For example, a crafting club, choir, or cooking class can give them a sense of belonging. As long as the group is supportive and not overly competitive, Cancers can thrive in such settings, bonding over shared interests.

Managing Emotions Through Creative Outlets

Because Cancer can experience deep or shifting feelings, a hobby can be a healthy outlet. Painting, drawing, journaling, or even playing an instrument can serve as ways to release stress or sadness. Instead of holding emotions inside, they have a safe place to put them.

This emotional expression can also yield positive results if they turn a hobby into something more formal, like showcasing art or performing music. While some Cancers prefer to keep their talents private, others might find joy in sharing with an appreciative audience, especially if the environment feels encouraging rather than judgmental.

Hobbies That Reflect Caring Instincts

Many Cancers feel a pull to help others or to make the world a bit gentler. They might pick up hobbies that let them practice acts of kindness or support:

1. **Volunteering**: Helping in community projects such as soup kitchens or animal shelters.

2. **Organizing Fundraisers**: Using creative methods like baking or crafting to gather donations for a cause.

3. **Teaching Arts**: Guiding younger people in painting or crafts, offering a calm space for them to explore their own creativity.

These hobbies line up with the nurturing side of Cancer, channeling their empathy into real-world actions.

Learning New Skills

Though some Cancers prefer routines, they can also enjoy learning new things that enrich their lives. For instance, they might decide to learn a language so they can connect with people from other places. They might take up photography to capture special moments or start playing a musical instrument after watching a friend do so.

Their emotional involvement means they often do best if they truly care about the skill. If it connects to something meaningful—like capturing family memories through photography—they will likely stick to it longer. They can show patience and consistency when they see the value of the hobby in their everyday world.

Relaxing Hobbies for Stress Relief

On tough days, some hobbies can give Cancers immediate stress relief:

- **Coloring Books**: Focusing on simple designs can calm the mind.

- **Gentle Exercise**: Activities like easy yoga or stretching can lower tension.

- **Listening to Music**: Creating a personal playlist to match their mood.

- **Puzzles**: Solving jigsaws or crosswords can help them shift focus away from worries.

These types of activities are not about performing for others; they are about finding a moment of peace amid life's demands.

Adapting Hobbies to Changing Moods

Because Cancer's feelings can shift quickly, they might have to adjust their hobbies accordingly. On days when they feel energetic, they might tackle something active or social, like dancing or a group cooking class. On days when they feel quiet, they might prefer a simple, solitary craft.

Recognizing this pattern can help them avoid frustration. If they set strict schedules for hobbies they only enjoy sometimes, they might lose interest. Instead, they can keep a variety of options, choosing what suits their mood on any given day.

Collecting and Memory-Keeping

Some Cancers develop collections related to memories or history. They might collect photos of loved ones, postcards from places they've visited, or small antiques that remind them of the past. Arranging these items can feel like creating a window into their life story.

Memory-keeping can also include scrapbooking or digital photo albums. By organizing images and notes, they preserve moments that hold emotional meaning. This process can be soothing, letting them recall pleasant times and handle the sad ones in a gentle way.

Spiritual or Reflective Hobbies

Though not all Cancers are spiritual, some may find comfort in reflective activities. They might practice meditation, light gentle scents in a safe space, or try simple breathing exercises. These practices can be seen as hobbies because they do not require competition or outside judgment.

Reflective hobbies allow them to tune out the busy world and turn inward. They can think about their goals, relationships, or personal feelings in a quiet setting. This might lower anxiety and help them feel more balanced when they return to daily tasks.

Turning Hobbies into Side Projects

In some cases, Cancers might expand a favorite hobby into a small side project or home-based effort. For instance, if they love baking, they might offer cupcakes to neighbors or sell them at local events. If they excel at knitting, they could create custom scarves.

The key for Cancer is to keep a sense of ease in these projects. If they become too pressured or stressful, the hobby might lose its charm. They usually prefer a gentle pace rather than a rush for large-scale success. Maintaining a personal touch is more important than big achievements.

Social Media and Sharing Creations

With technology, it is easier than ever to share creations online. Some Cancers choose to post pictures of their artwork, crafts, or meals on social media. They might join groups that focus on a particular hobby, like painting or photography, and connect with others who share their interests.

However, because they can be sensitive, they should be cautious about negative comments. The online world can be harsh, and unkind words might sting. They can limit their exposure by focusing on supportive platforms or by posting only in groups with friendly guidelines. That way, they can share their work without feeling too vulnerable.

Involving Friends and Family

Cancers often like to include loved ones in their hobbies. They might plan a craft night with friends, asking everyone to bring a project to work on. Or they might gather the family for a board game session, picking a game that does not spark too much rivalry.

By doing this, they turn their hobbies into bonding moments. Even if the actual activity is simple, the shared laughter or conversation can strengthen connections. Cancer's caring spirit often wants to see everyone enjoying the activity together.

Finding Inspiration in Everyday Life

For a Cancer, inspiration can come from everyday scenes—sunlight through curtains, the color of a family member's eyes, or the pattern of raindrops on a window. Because they notice small details, they can incorporate these observations into their art, writing, or music.

They might keep a small notebook to jot down ideas when something moves them. Later, they can return to those notes and expand on them. This habit can help them stay inspired, even during busy weeks when they cannot devote much time to their hobbies.

Balancing Hobbies with Obligations

While hobbies are important, Cancers must also meet daily responsibilities—jobs, household tasks, or caring for others. Some might worry that taking time for themselves is selfish. In fact, setting aside moments for hobbies can recharge them, improving their ability to handle other tasks.

They can schedule short blocks of creative or relaxing time, whether that is 30 minutes of drawing before bed or an hour of music practice on weekends. By viewing this as part of self-care rather than a luxury, they can maintain a balance between what they need to do and what they love to do.

Overcoming Creative Blocks

Just like anyone, Cancers might experience times when they do not feel inspired. They could find themselves staring at a blank page or canvas, unsure how to proceed. When this happens, stepping away can help. They might take a walk, listen to uplifting music, or do a different hobby.

If the block is tied to strong emotions—such as sadness or worry—it might help to talk to a friend or write down the concern. Once the emotional weight is lifted, creativity might flow again. Patience is key, as forcing inspiration can lead to frustration.

Collaborative Efforts

Some Cancers thrive when they join forces with others on creative projects. They might pair up with a friend who writes music while they write lyrics, or co-create a piece of art for a community space. This allows them to share ideas and emotional insights, often leading to unique results.

The main thing is finding collaborators who respect Cancer's gentle style and do not push them to work faster or in a way that feels uncomfortable. If the atmosphere stays positive and everyone feels heard, it can be a fulfilling experience.

Documenting Growth in Skills

As they develop a hobby, Cancer might enjoy seeing their progress. They could keep old drawings or recordings to compare with newer ones. This can remind them how far they have come, even if the changes are subtle.

They do not need constant praise from others; however, a few kind words can encourage them to keep going. If they share a new poem with a friend and receive a thoughtful comment, it might motivate them to write more. They also appreciate constructive advice, as long as it is given gently.

Seeking Peace in Crafts and Hobbies

Above all, hobbies for Cancer often serve as a way to find calm in a busy world. Whether it is coloring, crocheting, cooking, or dancing, these activities provide a mini-retreat from stress. They can let go of worries for a while and focus on something positive.

This sense of calm can carry over into the rest of their life. After spending an hour playing an instrument or working on a scrapbook, they may feel more balanced. This is especially helpful on days when emotional waves are strong, and they need a gentle anchor.

Ideas for Hobbies a Cancer Might Try

Handmade Candles: Mixing scents that feel cozy or comforting.

Simple Gardening: Growing herbs in a window box or caring for a few potted flowers.

Reading Clubs: Sharing insights about novels that focus on emotional themes.

Photography: Capturing family moments or nature scenes that speak to them.

Creative Journaling: Combining art, writing, and personal reflection in one place.

Traveling as a Hobby

Not all Cancers like the idea of long journeys (especially if it disrupts their sense of home), but some do enjoy short trips or day tours to interesting spots. They might take a train ride to a nearby town or visit a historical site. During these trips, they often collect photos or small souvenirs.

Once they return, they might use those items for crafts or create a photo collage that reminds them of the experience. This blends their love of memory-keeping with a mild taste for exploration. As long as they have a comfortable place to stay and feel safe, such trips can inspire new creative projects.

Helping Others Find Their Talents

Because Cancers are so supportive, they may encourage friends or children to explore their own hobbies. They might help someone pick out art supplies or offer tips for cooking a tasty meal. If they notice a friend wants to try sewing, they might lend them a machine or share easy starter patterns.

By helping others find enjoyment in creativity, Cancers spread warmth in their social circle. They do not typically force their own hobbies on people but offer guidance when asked. If someone shows interest, Cancer is happy to provide a gentle nudge in the right direction.

Keeping Hobbies Fun, Not Stressful

One potential pitfall is turning a hobby into a source of stress by setting very high expectations. If a Cancer starts to feel pressured to be perfect, the activity loses its relaxing benefit. It is important for them to remember that hobbies are supposed to be enjoyable, not an added burden.

They might need to remind themselves, "It's okay if this painting is not flawless," or "I'm making this knit scarf for fun, not to impress anyone." Letting go of harsh self-criticism can keep the hobby pleasant and keep their confidence strong.

Conclusion

For Cancer, creativity and hobbies are often personal expressions of emotion. Whether through painting, cooking, music, or gentle outdoor activities, they pour parts of themselves into what they do. These outlets can soothe their sensitive side, help them handle stress, and bring moments of joy and fulfillment.

By choosing hobbies that match their caring spirit and allowing themselves the freedom to explore without too much self-pressure, they can find lasting satisfaction. In this way, their interests become an extension of the warm, imaginative world they carry within, bridging the gap between inner feelings and outer expression.

CHAPTER 8: DAILY ROUTINES AND HABITS

Every person has daily routines, but for Cancer, these routines can be tied closely to emotional well-being. In this chapter, we will explore the ways Cancers typically structure their day, from morning to night, and how they handle tasks like meals, chores, personal care, and relaxation. We will also look at how their natural rhythms and moods might shape their habits and how they find balance in everyday life.

The Importance of Morning Calm

Many Cancers prefer a slow and gentle start to the day if possible. Jumping out of bed and rushing through chores can leave them feeling scattered. If they have time, they might sit quietly with a warm drink, letting themselves wake up at a comfortable pace.

Some might use this time to read a few pages of a book, check in with loved ones by message, or do mild stretches. This sets a calm tone, helping them face the tasks ahead without feeling anxious. Of course, if they must hurry to school or work, they may try to at least take a moment to breathe before stepping out the door.

Planning the Day Ahead

Cancers often feel more at ease when they have a loose plan. They might keep a journal or small planner to write down what needs to be done—errands, appointments, or tasks at work. Knowing what to expect can lower the chance of feeling overwhelmed.

At the same time, they might not like overly strict schedules that leave no room for flexibility. Emotional shifts can happen, so having a bit of wiggle room allows them to adjust if they are feeling tired or if something unexpected comes up.

A Balanced Approach to Chores

Because they tend to value a cozy environment, Cancers usually keep their living space neat. They might prefer to do a little cleaning each day rather than a big cleanup once in a while. For example, they might spend 15 minutes tidying the kitchen or wiping surfaces rather than letting messes grow.

However, they can also become stressed if chores pile up. If they live with others, they may ask for shared help so they do not feel the entire burden. Delegating tasks, like having children or roommates put away their own things, can keep balance and prevent Cancer from feeling overwhelmed.

Healthy Eating Routines

Many Cancers view food as a source of comfort. They might plan simple, home-cooked meals that remind them of family traditions or favorite childhood dishes. They could also be mindful of nutrition if they worry about health.

Eating regular meals can help them avoid dips in mood caused by hunger. Skipping meals or eating on the run might lead them to feel uneasy. They prefer to sit down at a table and take time to enjoy the food. Even a quick breakfast can feel more grounded if they pause to appreciate it.

Scheduling Breaks During the Day

If they have a job or a day full of errands, Cancers do well when they schedule small breaks. This could be a short walk outside, a brief chat with a friend, or simply closing their eyes and breathing deeply for a minute.

These breaks let them mentally recharge. Since they can absorb tension from their surroundings, stepping away from noise or busy places can bring relief. If they skip breaks, they might become irritable or tired without realizing why.

Managing Energy Levels

Cancers can have fluctuating energy throughout the day. In the morning, some might feel energetic and ready to tackle tasks, while others move more slowly until late morning. By afternoon, they could need a short rest or snack to keep going.

Listening to these natural peaks and dips helps them plan tasks more effectively. They might schedule more demanding work during their high-energy times and simpler tasks or rest during low-energy periods. This approach can boost overall productivity and prevent burnout.

Fitting Personal Care into the Routine

Self-care is crucial for a sign that takes on so many emotions. Cancers might include activities like a warm bath, skincare steps, or quiet reading time in their daily or weekly routine. These moments remind them to look after their own well-being instead of just caring for everyone else.

Some may also find calm in lighting gentle scents or keeping soft lighting in the bathroom or bedroom. Little touches like candles, soothing music, or soft pillows can help them feel safe and relaxed. As long as it does not become a chore, these habits can bring a sense of peace.

Work or School Schedules

Many Cancers adapt their day around work or school needs. They can be punctual and organized if they understand how their efforts fit into a bigger goal. They might arrive early to set up their workspace or check messages before the rush starts.

If the job or school day is hectic, they may look forward to returning home in the evening, where they can slip into a more relaxed routine. During busy seasons, they might need to remind themselves to set boundaries, like not answering work emails late into the night, to keep from feeling drained.

Evening Wind-Down

By the end of the day, Cancers often benefit from a gentle wind-down routine. This could mean dimming the lights, putting on soft music, or changing into comfortable clothes. If they live with others, they might chat about the day's events, or they might prefer a bit of alone time first.

Some might also enjoy writing in a notebook to reflect on what happened and plan for tomorrow. This reflection can help clear the mind, making sleep easier. Cancers who skip this wind-down phase might find themselves lying awake with thoughts swirling, so a consistent evening pattern can make a big difference.

Sleep Habits

Cancers usually need enough sleep to feel balanced. Lack of rest can magnify their sensitivities, making them more prone to moodiness. They often like to create a cozy sleeping environment—maybe soft sheets, a preferred pillow, or light fabric that keeps them at a comfortable temperature.

For better rest, they might avoid harsh TV shows right before bed or might turn off electronic devices early. If they share a room with someone else, they often appreciate a partner who respects their desire for a calm sleeping space. Good sleep supports the emotional stability that is so important to them.

Handling Sudden Changes

Even with well-planned routines, life can present surprises—unexpected tasks, a sick family member, or last-minute invitations. Cancers can find sudden changes stressful, but they usually adapt if they have a bit of warning. They might re-check their schedule or talk to someone to figure out a new plan.

They might also need emotional support in such moments, especially if the change affects a loved one. A few comforting words from a friend or partner can make all the difference, helping them accept the new situation and adjust their day accordingly.

Family-Centered Routines

In families, Cancer parents or guardians often create routines that build a sense of closeness. This can include set meal times, bedtime stories, or regular chores for each family member. They might also like weekly dinners or simple family gatherings where everyone shares a bit about their day.

Keeping these routines stable can give children a feeling of security. However, Cancer adults must be careful not to become too rigid. If they over-focus on tradition, they might not leave room for spontaneous fun. Balancing structure with flexibility helps keep the atmosphere positive.

Balancing Alone Time and Together Time

While Cancer loves family and friends, they also need quiet moments. Finding that balance might involve setting aside a half-hour in the evening to read alone or take a gentle walk. If they live with many people, they might designate a small corner of the house as a personal retreat space.

This does not mean they do not want others around. It means they need occasional breaks from constant interaction. Explaining this need to loved ones can prevent misunderstandings. When they return to group settings, they can be more present and open.

Managing Technology Use

With devices available day and night, Cancers might need to set guidelines for themselves. For instance, they could decide to turn off their phone or step away from social media after a certain hour. Constant notifications can disrupt their sense of calm, especially if they are prone to picking up on stressful news or negative interactions online.

By limiting screen time, they allow themselves to focus on real-life tasks, hobbies, or personal interactions. This can improve their mood and help them get better rest, supporting a healthier routine overall.

Health and Exercise

Not all Cancers are big fans of intense workouts, but they do benefit from gentle physical activities. They might try walks, low-impact aerobics, or relaxed cycling. Water-based exercise, like swimming or aqua aerobics, can feel refreshing, fitting their water sign nature.

They may also keep a close eye on nutrition if they feel it affects their moods or energy. They might choose meals that are satisfying yet balanced, paying attention to how different foods make them feel. Eating enough fruits, vegetables, and hydration can keep their minds clearer, helping them stay steady through the day.

Flexible Routines on Weekends

Many Cancers enjoy weekends or days off as times to slow down further. They might sleep a bit later or enjoy a calm breakfast with family. If they have big chores to do, they might spread them out so the entire day is not consumed by tasks.

They might also plan a simple outing—like visiting a local market or a friend's house—if it does not feel too rushed. By keeping these plans relaxed, they preserve the sense of rest and renewal that free days can bring.

Evening Activities and Entertainment

When it comes to entertainment, Cancers might choose cozy or heartwarming shows over loud, action-packed ones. They like stories that touch on family themes, personal growth, or gentle humor. Watching something that resonates with their caring side can leave them feeling uplifted.

Other times, they might prefer reading a book or listening to music that matches the day's mood. If they have friends over, they might suggest board games or group conversations rather than wild parties. These choices reflect their desire for emotional safety and connection.

Adjusting Routines for Life Changes

Major life changes—like moving to a new home, having a child, or switching jobs—can throw routines off balance. Cancers may feel disoriented if their usual patterns vanish overnight. They might cope by slowly building new habits in the new environment.

For example, if they move to a different house, they may start by setting up a comfortable bedroom, then plan a new route to work, and finally see how they can adapt mealtime routines. Taking it step by step helps them feel more secure, preventing the stress from becoming overwhelming.

Balancing Generosity with Personal Needs

A big part of Cancer's daily life can involve helping others. They might take care of children, support older family members, or look after pets. They might also be the friend people call for advice. While this is part of their nature, it can drain them if they do not set boundaries.

They might schedule personal breaks, even if it is just 10 minutes to sip tea without interruption. If they never get a moment alone, they risk becoming irritable or exhausted. By pacing themselves, they can continue to care for loved ones without neglecting their own well-being.

Coping with Stressful Days

Even with the best routines, stressful days happen. A Cancer might come home feeling anxious or on edge after dealing with conflicts or unexpected problems. In these moments, having a familiar set of steps can be calming.

They might put away their belongings neatly, change into comfortable clothes, and do a short relaxation technique—like breathing in for four counts, holding for four, and releasing for four. They could also talk with a trusted friend or partner about what happened. Sharing the worry can lighten the load, preventing it from following them into the night.

Social Commitments and Scheduling

Cancers often like to plan social visits in advance so they can prepare emotionally and practically. Sudden invitations might cause them to hesitate, especially if they are already feeling tired. If they do agree to spontaneous plans, they might need to confirm the details—where, when, who will be there—so they can visualize the event and feel comfortable about it.

They might also limit the number of social events in a week. Going out every night can leave them drained, so they might plan one or two gatherings and keep other evenings free for rest. This helps them avoid burnout and maintain their sense of calm.

Pets and Daily Routines

Many Cancers love pets because they provide warm companionship. Pets also give structure to a Cancer's day—regular feeding times, walks, or play sessions. This can be a comforting cycle, and the unconditional affection from an animal can ease daily stress.

If they have a dog, they might relish short walks that double as quiet thinking time. If they have a cat, they might enjoy sharing a cozy corner on the sofa. For fish or small animals, just observing them can be relaxing. Caring for a pet aligns with Cancer's nurturing spirit, though they must ensure they have enough time to do so properly.

Keeping a Home Calendar

A physical calendar in the kitchen or living room can help the entire household stay organized. It might show important dates, appointments, or reminders. A Cancer might decorate it with warm colors or pictures to make it visually pleasing.

Having this shared calendar means everyone knows the plan, lowering confusion or last-minute chaos. It also lets Cancer see the bigger picture: birthdays, family visits, or routine checkups. They can feel more in control of upcoming events, which supports their desire for stability.

Handling Overcommitment

Cancers might find themselves saying "yes" to too many requests—hosting gatherings, driving relatives around, or helping friends move. They do this because they care and want to be helpful. But if they take on too much, they may run out of energy.

They must practice gently saying, "I'm sorry, but I can't manage that right now." This is not about rejecting others; it is about protecting their own health. If they overdo it, they might become resentful, which harms relationships. By balancing kindness toward others with kindness toward themselves, they can maintain a healthy routine.

Seasonal Adjustments

Cancers are sometimes affected by changes in seasons. During colder months, they might spend more time indoors, focusing on cooking or cozy indoor routines. Warmer months might inspire them to take evening walks or do light gardening.

They might also notice their moods shift with the weather. If dark, chilly days bring down their spirits, they can add more uplifting elements to their home—brighter lights, indoor plants, or cheerful music. During sunny times, they can open windows or step outside more often. Adjusting their daily habits to the season can keep them feeling balanced year-round.

Celebrating Small Wins in Daily Life

Though they are careful with time, Cancers can find small ways to honor achievements or good moments. They might treat themselves to a favorite tea or take a relaxing bath when something goes well. They might also share their happiness with loved ones, perhaps by cooking something special or writing a thankful note.

Recognizing these positive moments, even if briefly, helps them maintain an upbeat outlook and reminds them that daily life includes successes as well as challenges. This practice keeps them going during tougher times and ensures they do not overlook the bright spots.

Balancing Structure and Spontaneity

While routine is comforting, too much predictability might feel dull. Occasionally, a Cancer might surprise their household by trying a new dish, rearranging furniture, or planning a short outing. These small changes can keep life interesting without causing undue stress.

The key is finding a middle ground. If everything is always the same, there can be boredom. If everything is always changing, Cancer might feel unsettled. Adapting routines now and then can keep them fresh, as long as it is done thoughtfully.

Routines for Emotional Well-Being

Beyond chores and schedules, Cancer might establish habits specifically for emotional care. This could be a daily gratitude list, where they note a few things that went right. Or it could be a weekly check-in with a close friend to talk about feelings.

They might also practice gentle self-talk when they wake up or before bed. For instance, quietly reminding themselves, "I am safe, and I can handle the day ahead," can set a positive tone. These small habits make a big difference in a sign that feels emotions so strongly.

CHAPTER 9: COMMUNICATION STYLES

Communication can show a lot about a person's personality. For Cancer, the way they speak, listen, and respond is shaped by a caring nature and a focus on emotions. In this chapter, we will look at how Cancer tends to communicate in different parts of life—among friends, at work, in family settings, and in moments of conflict. We will also explore how they might handle misunderstandings or stressful talks, and how they can build stronger connections through clear dialogue.

Softness and Sensitivity

One of the most noticeable things about Cancer's communication is a gentle touch. They often choose words with care, wanting to avoid harming someone's feelings. This is not because they are timid, but rather because they value emotional safety for everyone involved. Even when they are upset, they might try to keep their tone calm or quiet, especially in a face-to-face talk.

However, this gentleness can also mean they hold back if they sense the other person is not ready to hear certain truths. They might sugarcoat messages to avoid conflict. At times, people who prefer direct conversation could misread this approach as being vague. Cancer's softness can be a strength, but they also learn that sometimes honest clarity is more helpful than avoiding the issue.

Attentive Listening

Cancers do not just talk—they listen. In fact, they might show interest in the other person's story or concerns before mentioning their own. Their eyes and facial expressions often show empathy, as if they are absorbing every detail. Friends or coworkers might notice that a Cancer can recall small facts mentioned days earlier, like a personal worry or a special date.

This attentive style helps people feel seen and understood. It can build trust, since the other person senses that Cancer genuinely cares about what they are saying. However, this can also lead to emotional overload if Cancer takes in too many heavy stories without a break. Finding a balance—being caring but not carrying all the weight—is an ongoing skill.

The Need for Emotional Safety

Before opening up fully, Cancer wants to feel safe. This desire shapes their communication in many ways. In a new friendship, they might start by sharing small bits of themselves, watching to see how the other person reacts. If the person seems kind and trustworthy, Cancer may reveal deeper thoughts or more personal stories.

On the flip side, if they sense judgment, they might retreat or switch topics. This can appear as shyness or aloofness, but usually it is just self-protection. They do not want to risk pouring out their feelings only to be mocked or dismissed. Over time, once trust is built, they can be quite expressive, letting their warmth and humor shine.

Body Language and Tone

Cancers might lean in when you speak, nod in agreement, or mirror your expressions. They are good at using eye contact to show genuine interest, though if they feel nervous, they could glance down or to the side. Their tone of voice tends to be soothing or gentle when things are calm.

However, if they are hurt or angry, their tone can shift rapidly. Some may speak in a hushed tone, as though they do not want everyone to overhear the conflict. Others might become sharper or take on a defensive posture, folding their arms or turning their body away. Recognizing these subtle signs can help loved ones see when a Cancer is upset.

Communication in Group Settings

When in a group—such as a classroom, office meeting, or party—Cancer might not rush to speak up right away. They may observe the atmosphere first. This makes them good at reading the room, spotting who is comfortable and who might feel left out.

Once they do speak, they might offer thoughtful points or ask questions that draw quieter folks in. Because they care about harmony, they often try to involve everyone, hoping to keep the mood positive. If the group is loud or aggressive, Cancer might slip into the background, preferring not to get involved in heated debates.

Conflict Resolution and Tough Talks

Although they value peace, conflicts happen. A Cancer might deal with conflict by trying to stay calm and keep the tone gentle. They may encourage a one-on-one conversation rather than hashing everything out in front of an audience. This private setting helps them feel safer, and it can also reduce tension.

If the other person is yelling or attacking, a Cancer could become overwhelmed. Some might tear up, while others might retreat and stop talking. Learning to hold their ground can be a challenge. Over time, they might learn phrases like, "I'm hearing what you say, but I need a moment to think before I respond," to give themselves space to breathe.

Written Communication

Texts, emails, and social media messages can sometimes hide tone and feeling. For a Cancer, who places great importance on the emotional side of words, this can be tricky. They might use emojis or polite language to make sure they sound friendly. They might worry if a message could be taken the wrong way.

If a text seems cold or short, they might read too much into it, fearing the other person is upset. They do better when there is a clear sign of warmth in written notes—like a short greeting, a sign-off with care, or a small personal comment. This helps them feel that the bond is strong, even without face-to-face interaction.

Communication in Romantic Relationships

In love, Cancer's communication style centers on empathy and emotional sharing. They want to know their partner's feelings and will likely ask questions like, "How was your day, really?" or "You seem worried—do you want to talk about it?" They might send caring messages throughout the day if they know their partner is facing stress.

However, their strong emotional focus can lead to overthinking. If a partner does not reply quickly, a Cancer may worry the bond is breaking. Reassurance helps them feel secure. A few warm words—like "I appreciate you" or "I'm proud of you"—can keep them steady. They often respond by returning that kindness in their own gentle way.

Communication with Family

Because family is important to Cancer, the way they talk at home can be both tender and protective. They might use soft tones and encouraging words, especially with children. They pay attention to each family member's mood and try to address problems before they grow too big.

When faced with family disagreements, they might play the role of mediator, helping sides understand each other. However, if the conflict involves them personally, they may need more time to process emotions. They could become quiet and reflective, sorting out their thoughts before discussing solutions. Family members who learn to give them a bit of space see that eventually, Cancer opens up with calm honesty.

Handling Gossip or Negative Talk

Cancers typically avoid gossip or petty negativity. If coworkers or friends start talking badly about someone, a Cancer might feel uncomfortable. They may try to steer the conversation to something kinder or simply remove themselves from the chat. They dislike seeing anyone unfairly judged.

If they become the subject of gossip, they can feel hurt deeply. They might withdraw from the group, not wanting to confront the issue head-on. Over time, they can learn that speaking up—saying "This is hurtful" or "I'd rather discuss this face to face"—can be healthier. Still, they prefer respectful, calm exchanges whenever possible.

Communicating Needs and Boundaries

It can be hard for Cancer to state their own needs, especially if they worry about inconveniencing others. They might hope people will just notice they are overwhelmed or sad. Unfortunately, not everyone sees these subtle signs. This can lead to Cancer feeling ignored or unappreciated.

Learning to voice boundaries is an important step. For example, if they need personal time to rest, they can say, "I'm sorry, but I can't talk right now. I need a moment alone." Or if they feel pressured to take on too many tasks, they can gently explain, "I'd love to help, but my schedule is already full." These clear statements prevent misunderstandings and protect their emotional energy.

Politeness vs. Authenticity

Because Cancer wants to keep harmony, they might say something is "fine" even if it is not. This politeness can mask real feelings. While they might think they are keeping peace, it can cause confusion later when the truth surfaces. Learning to be tactful yet honest is a skill that helps them avoid building hidden resentment.

In friendly or professional settings, a Cancer might say, "I see your point," even if they disagree, just to keep things smooth. But a healthier approach might be politely expressing their view: "I understand your perspective, but I feel differently. Here's why." This balanced honesty can be tough at first, but it fosters genuine respect.

Communication Triggers

Certain topics might trigger strong emotions in Cancer. These could involve family conflicts, betrayals of trust, or anything that challenges their sense of security. If someone brings up a sensitive issue without warning, Cancer might shut down or react emotionally.

Friends or partners who know these triggers can approach them with understanding. They might say, "I want to discuss this serious topic—are you in a good place to talk right now?" This courtesy gives Cancer a chance to get ready emotionally. When they feel prepared, they are more willing to open up rather than hiding.

Using Humor

Cancers can have a gentle sense of humor that brings people closer. They often use light jokes, playful teasing (in a kind way), or funny stories from daily life. This gentle laughter can break tension in a group or show solidarity when someone feels awkward.

However, they rarely enjoy harsh or mean jokes. If a conversation shifts to mocking someone's flaws, Cancer may withdraw or try to change the subject. They prefer humor that makes people smile without hurtful jabs. In a close group of friends, they might reveal a silly, fun side, telling stories in a lively manner that draws everyone in.

Recognizing Indirect Cues

Some Cancers communicate in indirect ways. They might show they are upset by giving short answers or looking away rather than stating outright, "I'm hurt." They might also reveal their needs through gestures—like tidying the house more than usual if they are stressed, or cooking a special meal when they want affection.

Friends and family who pick up on these subtle cues can respond with gentle questions: "I notice you've been quiet today—are you okay?" or "You've been working non-stop; do you need help?" This approach tells Cancer that someone sees their unspoken signals and cares enough to check in. Over time, Cancer may learn to be more direct, but in the meantime, supportive loved ones can help by noticing these hints.

Talking with Children

When interacting with children, Cancer tends to speak calmly and with empathy. They might kneel down to a child's level or keep eye contact to show full attention. If a child is upset, a Cancer adult might softly ask, "Can you tell me why you're sad?" instead of demanding an answer. This approach helps kids feel safe sharing emotions.

They also prefer constructive guidance rather than scolding. If a child does something wrong, they might explain gently, "That action made your friend feel bad. How can we fix this?" By focusing on understanding feelings, they hope to teach empathy. Over time, these caring talks can form a strong emotional bond with the children in their life.

Professional Communication and Clarity

In the workplace, Cancer may rely on a calm, polite manner. They often take care in writing emails, double-checking for a friendly tone and correct grammar. They might address coworkers by name, include small friendly greetings, and end with a polite sign-off. This attention to detail can help them form good relationships in a job setting.

They do need to watch out for over-apologizing or downplaying their work. If they contributed a strong idea, they should feel comfortable stating it with confidence: "I propose we try this approach because…" rather than "Maybe this is silly, but…" Being clear and self-assured helps colleagues see their genuine value.

Dealing with Interruptions

If a conversation partner is impatient or talks over them, a Cancer might go quiet. This can be frustrating, especially if they had something important to say. They may feel it is pointless to fight for the floor. Later, they might regret not speaking up.

One strategy is politely asserting, "Excuse me, I'd like to finish my thought," or holding up a hand gently to indicate they have more to say. This small action can remind the other person to pause. Though it might feel uncomfortable at first, it often leads to more balanced communication.

Encouraging Openness

Cancers enjoy conversations that go beyond surface topics. They might ask deeper questions about someone's past, dreams, or feelings. This does not mean prying, but rather showing genuine curiosity. If the other person is open, they can have meaningful talks that strengthen their bond.

If the other person is reserved, Cancer may back off, not wanting to push. They could say, "It's okay if you don't feel like sharing right now," showing respect for boundaries. Usually, this gentle invitation can help the other person feel safe enough to open up in their own time.

Learning from Mistakes in Communication

No one communicates perfectly all the time. Cancers might sometimes let emotions run high and say things they regret. They might also keep quiet when a discussion needed their input. Reflecting on these moments can help them do better next time.

They might apologize if they spoke harshly, saying something like, "I'm sorry for raising my voice. I was overwhelmed." Or they could let someone know, "I realize I was silent when you needed my help. I want to be more supportive in the future." Admitting missteps and attempting to improve fosters trust and growth in relationships.

Adapting to Others' Styles

Not everyone shares Cancer's approach. Some folks are very direct, while others might be more logical and less emotional. Cancers can learn to adapt by noticing how the other person prefers to talk. If the other person wants concise facts, Cancer might cut back on too many emotional details. If the other person enjoys sharing feelings, Cancer can match that level of openness.

This does not mean changing who they are; it just means fine-tuning their style so the message lands well. Healthy communication often involves meeting halfway. Cancers can keep their warmth but also offer more structure or straightforward points when dealing with someone who likes quick, clear statements.

Public Speaking

Public speaking can be a challenge for some Cancers if they dislike crowds or fear harsh judgment. But if they see it as a chance to share helpful information, they can tap into their caring side. They might prepare notes carefully, focusing on how to connect with the audience's emotions rather than just listing facts.

Even a shy Cancer can do well once they find a comfortable approach—perhaps including a brief personal story or a gentle tone to calm the room. Afterward, they may feel relieved but also proud that they pushed through their hesitation. It helps to practice ahead of time and maybe get feedback from a close friend.

Social Media Presence

Many Cancers keep a warm, friendly tone online. They might share photos of family, homemade meals, or uplifting messages. They could also engage with friends' posts by leaving kind comments. However, if online spaces become too negative or argumentative, they might prefer to step away rather than fight.

They tend to avoid posting harsh opinions or getting into long debates. If a friend or stranger tries to pick a fight, Cancer might respond politely once, then choose to exit the conversation if it becomes mean. They appreciate digital interactions that mirror their values of kindness and respect.

Handling Silence

Silence in a conversation can make Cancer uneasy if they assume it means the other person is upset. Yet silence can also be comfortable, especially if both sides understand each other. In close relationships, a quiet moment does not have to feel awkward. It can be a shared pause for thoughts or rest.

Sometimes, Cancer might fill the silence with small talk or apologetic comments. Over time, they can learn that silence can be a natural part of communication. It can allow emotions to settle, giving each person a moment to breathe before speaking again.

Encouraging Healthier Communication in Others

Cancers, by their caring nature, can gently guide others to be more aware of feelings. They might model active listening, paraphrasing what the other person said to show understanding. They could also encourage more respectful behavior in a group by saying something like, "Let's hear everyone's ideas before we decide."

Though they do not force people to change, their soft approach can influence the overall tone of a conversation. They might offer constructive feedback: "I notice we interrupt each other a lot. Maybe we can take turns speaking?" This approach can improve group dynamics without causing resentment.

Communication Breakdowns

Sometimes, misunderstandings happen despite best efforts. A Cancer could find that a coworker misread their gentle tone as lack of confidence, or a friend felt ignored because Cancer was too subtle in showing empathy. When this happens, clearing up confusion early is best.

They can reach out privately, saying, "I sense something is off between us. Can we talk about it?" This direct move can prevent grudges from building. By listening calmly and explaining their side, they can find a solution that respects both perspectives.

Learning to Speak on Their Own Behalf

Advocating for themselves does not always come naturally to Cancer. They might want a raise, but fear they do not deserve it, or they might have an idea but worry it is not good enough. Learning to voice their abilities can feel uncomfortable.

A useful tip is to list facts: "I've met my deadlines and helped with extra tasks, so I believe a raise is fair," or "My plan might work well because it is cost-effective." Stating clear points rather than focusing on emotions can help them speak on their own behalf with greater confidence.

Supporting Others Through Communication

Cancers thrive when they can offer comfort. If a friend is going through a hard time, they might say, "I'm here for you. Tell me whatever you feel ready to share." They will usually give the friend room to talk, nodding or making small supportive sounds. They might also respond with words like, "That sounds tough," or "I understand why you feel that way," to validate the friend's experience.

They do need to watch out for over-involvement. If they absorb all the friend's troubles, they might become emotionally worn. Setting gentle limits—like taking a break after a long talk or suggesting the friend also speak to a counselor—can preserve their mental and emotional strength.

CHAPTER 10: CHALLENGES AND WEAKNESSES

No sign is perfect, and Cancer is no exception. Though they bring kindness and depth of feeling to many parts of life, they also face certain stumbling blocks. In this chapter, we will explore the typical challenges or weaknesses linked to the Cancer sign. We will look at how these hurdles show up in daily life, relationships, and emotional health. We will also consider ways to manage them without losing the caring nature that defines Cancer.

Over-Sensitivity

Perhaps the most commonly mentioned challenge for Cancer is that they can be quite sensitive. This means they feel joy strongly, but they also feel pain or criticism in an intense way. A small slight—like a coworker forgetting to greet them—can linger in their thoughts all day. They might worry the person dislikes them.

This over-sensitivity can lead to misreading situations. Sometimes, the coworker simply got busy and did not notice anyone else. Learning to pause before assuming the worst can be helpful. Asking a kind question, such as "Everything okay today?" might uncover a simple reason, preventing Cancer from hurting silently over a minor or unintended event.

Avoidance of Conflict

Cancer often prefers harmony. While this is a positive quality, it can turn into avoidance of conflict even when an issue needs to be addressed. They might pretend everything is fine to keep the peace, only to let resentments build inside.

Over time, these unspoken feelings can burst out at the wrong moment, surprising friends or partners who had no idea something was wrong. The challenge is to find a constructive way to handle disagreements early. Expressing concerns calmly, using phrases like "It bothers me when…" can head off bigger problems later.

Fear of Rejection

Because they value emotional security, Cancers can have a deep fear of being rejected or pushed away. This can cause them to hold back from forming new friendships or pursuing new opportunities, worried they might not be good enough. In a romantic sense, they might hesitate to speak up about their feelings, fearing the other person might not return them.

This fear can also appear in work situations—like not volunteering for a leadership role or new project. They might think, "Someone else is surely more qualified." The key is to remind themselves that no one is perfect. Taking small risks can show them that rejection is not the end of the world and that their abilities are often stronger than they assume.

Holding onto the Past

Memories, both happy and sad, stay close to Cancer's heart. This can be a lovely trait, but it can also cause problems if they cannot move forward from hurtful events. A betrayal or painful breakup might stay in their minds for months or years, shaping how they trust others.

This challenge sometimes leads them to compare new experiences or relationships to past ones, expecting the same bad outcome. Learning to see each situation as unique can help. Therapy, journaling, or supportive talks with friends can ease the grip of old memories, allowing them to enjoy the present with less fear.

Mood Swings

Linked to the Moon's changing phases, Cancer's mood can shift quickly. One moment they might feel cheerful and engaged, the next moment they could withdraw or seem sad. These mood swings are not always tied to external events; they may reflect internal emotional currents.

While mood changes are normal, extreme swings can affect relationships. Loved ones might feel confused if they cannot predict when Cancer will be upbeat or down. Self-awareness is key. When Cancers notice a shift, they can say, "I'm feeling a bit low right now; I need a minute." This honesty helps people around them understand and respond kindly.

Over-Dependence on Home and Family

Home and family often bring comfort, but relying too heavily on these safe zones can limit Cancer's growth in other areas. If they refuse to venture beyond family circles, they might miss out on making new friends or exploring wider career options.

They could also place high emotional demands on family members, needing constant reassurance or support. This can lead to tension if relatives or close friends feel overwhelmed. Taking small steps—like joining a local group or visiting new places—can show them that security is not limited to just one place or set of people.

Difficulty Letting Go of Control

Though they appear gentle, some Cancers have a hidden desire to keep things under control, especially at home. They might arrange the furniture in a certain way and become upset if someone moves it. They could also want to direct how family events go, from the menu to the time schedule.

This urge stems from their wish for security. If everything is in order, they feel safer. But it can clash with others who want more freedom or spontaneity. Recognizing that some chaos is part of life, and that letting others help does not ruin security, can reduce these control issues.

Overprotectiveness

Cancer's protective instinct can become overprotective if taken too far. They might shield friends or family from normal life challenges, preventing them from learning and growing. They could also worry excessively about dangers, seeing threats where there are none.

This might strain their relationships, as people might feel smothered. A partner could feel that Cancer does not trust them to handle their own problems. Striking a balance—offering help but respecting others' independence—is key. By letting loved ones solve things themselves sometimes, Cancer still cares without limiting the other person's ability to stand on their own.

Tendency to Withdraw

When upset, many Cancers retreat into a mental or emotional "shell," like a crab. Instead of voicing their frustrations or sadness, they pull back, hoping others will notice and come to them with comfort. If no one does, they might feel lonely or resentful.

This pattern can cause misunderstandings because friends or family might not realize how serious the issue is. Learning to speak up with a clear statement—like "I'm upset and need some reassurance right now"—can prevent the confusion that arises from silent withdrawal. It can also help them process difficult feelings more effectively than stewing in them alone.

Passive-Aggressive Behavior

If a Cancer feels hurt but does not want to confront someone directly, they might show displeasure through indirect actions. For example, they might give someone the silent treatment, make small sarcastic remarks, or do tasks grudgingly. While they think they are communicating their unhappiness, the other person may only sense tension without understanding the root cause.

This behavior does not align with Cancer's true caring nature, but it can happen when they fear direct conflict. Working on calm honesty—saying something like, "I felt hurt when you said that,"—can spare both sides the confusion of hidden anger. It also fosters deeper trust.

Excessive Worry

Because they like to protect and care for people, Cancers can overthink potential dangers. They might worry about their loved ones' health, finances, or emotional well-being. This worry can become a cycle that robs them of peace, especially if they fixate on problems they cannot fix.

A helpful step is to separate concerns into two groups: things they can control and things they cannot. They might ask themselves, "Is there anything I can do to help this situation right now?" If the answer is no, they can try redirecting their thoughts or doing a calming activity. They can also share these worries with a trusted friend to gain a more balanced view.

Clinging to Familiar Routines

Routine gives Cancer comfort, but clinging too firmly can make them fear new experiences. They might stick to the same schedule, same foods, and same circle of friends for years. While this stability can be nice, it can also become stale if they never explore fresh options.

Even small changes—like trying a new dish, walking a new path, or signing up for a short class—can gently broaden their world. They might discover surprising joys or talents. They do not have to abandon all old routines, but mixing in a few new elements can keep life interesting and help them feel more adaptable.

Taking on Others' Emotions

Cancer's empathy is a gift, but it can be a weakness if they absorb too many emotional burdens. For example, if a friend is anxious, a Cancer might become anxious too, losing sleep over someone else's struggles. Over time, this can wear them down, leaving them depleted.

Learning emotional boundaries is vital. They can still listen and support, but they need to remember that each person's feelings are their own. Simple mental reminders—like silently telling themselves, "I can care without carrying this"—may help. Also, scheduling personal downtime after intense emotional talks can keep them from burning out.

Struggle with Self-Assertion

Some Cancers have trouble firmly stating their opinions or standing up for themselves in group settings. They may fear being perceived as pushy or cold. This can lead to missed opportunities or a sense of frustration when they watch others speak up.

A workaround is to focus on the common good. For instance, they can tell themselves that sharing their viewpoint might help the group reach a better decision. Knowing that their voice can bring balance or empathy to a discussion might give them the courage to speak. Over time, small steps build confidence.

Over-Reliance on External Validation

Cancers often look for signs that others value them, like kind words or gestures of appreciation. While it is natural to enjoy praise, relying too much on external approval can create emotional ups and downs. If they do not hear positive feedback, they might think they are unliked or failing.

Finding internal sources of validation—like setting personal goals and measuring progress for themselves—can stabilize this tendency. They can learn to tell themselves, "I did well because I worked hard and see my own improvement," rather than waiting for someone else to say it. This helps them stand firm even if external praise is missing.

Difficulty in Letting Others Solve Problems

Cancers like to help, but sometimes that can turn into a habit of solving problems for everyone. They might not realize that the other person wants to handle the issue on their own. By stepping in unasked, Cancer could undermine the other person's confidence or create dependency.

Asking, "Do you want my help or do you prefer to do this alone?" can clarify if intervention is welcome. If the answer is no, they should respect it. This might feel strange at first, but it allows for healthier relationships where each person has room to grow.

Dwelling on Negative Self-Talk

When things go wrong, a Cancer might blame themselves excessively. A single mistake can spiral into harsh thoughts like "I always mess up," or "I'm not good enough." This negative self-talk can lead to lower self-esteem, making it harder to take positive steps forward.

Tackling this habit involves spotting these unkind inner statements and replacing them with balanced facts: "I made one mistake, but I can fix it. It does not define me." Over time, they can shift the internal dialogue from self-blame to self-compassion, improving resilience.

Becoming Enmeshed in Others' Lives

Enmeshment occurs when personal boundaries blur, and Cancer might be at risk because of their desire for close bonds. They might track every detail of a friend's or partner's life, feeling strong emotions about those details. If the friend or partner steps away for a bit, Cancer might feel abandoned.

Healthy closeness still allows each person room to be an individual. Encouraging separate hobbies, friendships, or activities can help. Cancers might remind themselves that independence in a loved one does not mean rejection. Each person having their own space often strengthens, rather than weakens, the bond.

Underestimating Their Strength

Because they see themselves as gentle or soft, some Cancers might not recognize their own inner strength. They might label themselves weak because they cry easily or worry often. In reality, empathy and vulnerability can be signs of great courage—continuing to care deeply in a tough world is no small feat.

A helpful step is listing past challenges they overcame. This shows them that they have handled hard times, even if they felt shaky. It proves they have more resilience than they give themselves credit for. Embracing this strength can boost confidence without losing their gentle side.

Pessimism About the Future

If Cancers dwell on possible misfortunes or rejections, they may become pessimistic. They could expect things to go wrong rather than hoping for success. This mindset can cause them to miss good chances or sabotage their own goals.

Learning to balance caution with optimism is helpful. They can plan for potential issues while also envisioning positive outcomes. For instance, they could think, "Yes, something might go wrong, but I can handle it or find support. Meanwhile, there's also a chance everything will go well." This balanced view frees them from constant dread.

Insecurity in Social Settings

At a party or group event, a Cancer may question if they fit in. They might stand on the edges, observing, feeling uncertain if people actually want them there. If no one approaches them first, they might decide they are unwanted.

To counter this, they can remind themselves that many people feel shy, not just them. Taking a small initiative—like offering a greeting or asking about someone's day—can break the ice. Often, others are relieved when someone starts a friendly conversation. By focusing on making others comfortable, they might forget their own nerves.

Overspending When Emotional

Some Cancers soothe stress with small comforts, which might turn into overspending. They could buy items for their home or treat loved ones to gifts, trying to spark a sense of security. While the gesture is kind, it can create financial issues if it happens often.

Setting a simple budget and noticing emotional spending triggers can help. Before buying something unplanned, they might pause and ask, "Am I doing this because I truly need it, or because I'm upset about something?" If it is the latter, seeking emotional support in a healthier way—like a talk with a friend—may be better for both wallet and well-being.

Neglecting Their Own Goals

Because they prioritize others, Cancers sometimes push their own dreams aside. They might spend so much energy supporting a spouse or child that they never follow personal ambitions. Over time, this can lead to regret or a sense of lost identity.

It is not selfish to pursue personal goals alongside caring for loved ones. Scheduling small time blocks for their aspirations—like learning a new skill or working on a passion project—can keep them from losing sight of personal growth. Loved ones might even support them back, creating a more balanced dynamic.

Being Too Self-Critical of Emotional Reactions

Cancers can judge themselves harshly for feeling "too much." They might think it is wrong to cry at a movie or to get stressed over a small conflict. In truth, their emotional depth is part of who they are—it brings empathy and warmth to the world.

A better stance is accepting these feelings. Instead of scolding themselves, they can think, "This is part of me, and it has positive sides, too." If a reaction is overwhelming, they can explore calming techniques, but they do not need to shame themselves for being more sensitive than someone else.

Unclear Communication of Discomfort

When Cancer is uncomfortable, they might drop hints rather than state it plainly. For instance, if they want someone to leave their house, they might start cleaning up or yawning a lot rather than politely saying, "It's getting late, and I need rest." This can lead to confusion if the guest does not pick up on the hints.

Being more direct can feel strange at first, but it usually prevents awkwardness. A gentle statement like, "I'm sorry, but I need to wrap up for the night," is kinder in the long run than indirect signals that might be missed.

Comparing Themselves to Others

With social media showing everyone's best moments, a Cancer might compare their behind-the-scenes struggles to the polished images they see online. They could feel like a failure if they do not have the same successes or if their home is not as stylish as someone else's.

Reminding themselves that social media is often a highlight reel can help. Life is not always as perfect as it looks in photos. Each person has a unique path, so comparing can be unfair. Focusing on personal progress and the simple joys in daily life can lessen the pressure of these unhelpful comparisons.

Resistance to Accepting Help

Because they like to be the helpers, some Cancers feel uneasy accepting support from others. They might wave off offers of assistance, saying, "I'm fine," even if they are struggling. This can leave them feeling overwhelmed or lonely, when in fact people are willing to share the load.

Letting others help can strengthen bonds. Loved ones often want to return the care they receive. Whether it is a friend bringing a meal during a rough time or a sibling offering a ride, accepting help is not weakness. It is part of healthy, mutual support.

Viewing Breakdowns as Failures

Emotional breakdowns or crying spells can feel shameful to a Cancer who wants to appear steady and nurturing. Yet these moments are sometimes a natural release. Bottling up emotions too long can lead to bigger collapses later.

If a breakdown happens, it might be a sign that they have been carrying too much stress alone. Seeking a counselor or confiding in a friend can be a turning point. Rather than labeling it as failure, they can see it as a signal to set better boundaries or ask for assistance.

Concluding Thoughts on Cancer's Challenges

Every sign has its own hurdles, and for Cancer, many revolve around emotions, security, and the delicate balance between caring for others and caring for themselves. These weaknesses do not make a person flawed; they reveal areas where learning and growth can happen. By acknowledging over-sensitivity, fear of conflict, or old emotional burdens, a Cancer can become more mindful.

They can then find ways to keep their compassion without letting it trap them in unhealthy patterns. Whether it is learning to speak up sooner, set boundaries, or embrace new experiences, each step helps them refine the loving qualities at the heart of their sign. Through a bit of self-awareness and effort, Cancer can move beyond these obstacles, enjoying a fuller, happier life with the people they hold dear.

CHAPTER 11: STRENGTHS AND POTENTIAL

Cancer is often known for empathy and sensitivity, but there is much more to explore when we look at the positive side of this sign. Beneath any difficulties or worries, there is a strong set of abilities and possibilities waiting to be tapped. This chapter looks at the many strengths linked to Cancer. It also explains how these can grow into even greater potential when supported by awareness and practice.

We will explore various areas in which Cancer can shine: emotional intelligence, loyalty, creativity, leadership, and the capacity to influence others in a positive way. We will also discuss how Cancer can make use of these strengths in careers, personal relationships, and day-to-day life. By the end, it should be clear that a Cancer's true power often lies in the kind nature and close emotional bonds that are central to who they are.

The Value of Emotional Intelligence

One of Cancer's greatest strengths is emotional intelligence. They often sense the subtle feelings in a room, picking up on things that others might miss. This allows them to respond with compassion, easing conflicts or comforting someone who is upset. In many cases, people appreciate that Cancer seems to "just know" how they feel, even if they have not said it outright.

This is not a magical power. It comes from paying attention to body language, tone of voice, and tiny changes in expression. Cancers are typically curious about how people feel and want to understand their emotional state. This attentive approach can produce strong friendships and supportive work environments, because people feel truly seen.

If they choose, Cancers can build on this strength by studying more about emotional cues and healthy ways of responding. For instance, they can read books on active listening or take short classes on effective communication. By doing so, they take a natural talent and transform it into a well-developed ability.

Loyalty that Fosters Trust

Another key asset for Cancer is loyalty. When they commit to someone—a friend, a partner, or a cause—they tend to stick with that commitment through thick and thin. Friends often say that once they have a Cancer on their side, they can count on that person to show up, even during tough times.

This loyalty builds trust. People around Cancer might feel safe sharing secrets or personal worries, knowing that Cancer will not betray them. In a work setting, managers and colleagues value Cancer's dependability, whether it is meeting deadlines or stepping up to help a struggling teammate.

However, loyalty can go further than just showing up. A strong sense of dedication means Cancers can stand up for what they believe in, defend those who are treated unfairly, and put real effort into projects or relationships that matter to them. This level of trustworthiness can lead to leadership roles, because others feel secure under their guidance.

Creativity and a Rich Inner World

Cancer's imagination can be quite powerful. Their sensitivity to detail and emotion gives them a special viewpoint. In creative tasks, they may conjure images, words, or music that resonate with deep feelings. Whether they paint, write poems, or compose tunes, the result can touch the hearts of those who see or hear it.

This creativity does not have to be limited to art. It might show up as finding inventive ways to solve issues at work, planning an event with a unique theme, or decorating a living space to make it feel cozy. Because they tie their feelings to what they create, Cancers often produce outcomes that feel genuine. People may sense that the result is not just a routine job but something with personal meaning behind it.

Tapping into this creative side can open many doors. It could lead to side pursuits, like crafting or design, that bring satisfaction and even some extra income. Or it could allow a Cancer to shine in a professional setting where new ideas are valued. With the willingness to explore their imaginations more, they can find fresh paths for growth.

Nurturing Leadership Qualities

When many people think of leadership, they might picture loud or demanding types. But Cancer brings a different style of guidance, which can be equally effective. This sign's nurturing approach can unite teams in a warm way. Because they care about each person's emotional health, they may notice if someone is quiet or overwhelmed, then step in with support or gentle advice.

Over time, this can build team spirit. People who feel appreciated tend to work better together, share ideas freely, and trust each other. Cancers can excel as team leads, managers, or mentors if they trust in their empathetic qualities. They do not have to become someone they are not; they can lead by showing kindness, offering clear goals, and being available when someone needs a guiding hand.

Such nurturing leadership can also shine at home, where a Cancer might coordinate family schedules, settle disputes calmly, and encourage each family member to grow in their own way. Even in friend groups, a Cancer can be the one who pulls everyone together, plans get-togethers, or makes sure no one is left out.

Resilience Hidden Behind Sensitivity

Though they might appear delicate, Cancers often have a deep well of resilience. Life can deliver challenges—family issues, financial stress, or heartbreak—but Cancers tend to keep going. Part of their strength comes from the support they build around them. They know how to form close ties that become safety nets in bad times.

Also, their emotional approach can actually help them heal. Instead of ignoring sadness or stress, they often face it head-on, even if it feels overwhelming. Over time, this can lead to personal growth. By allowing feelings to flow, they avoid bottling everything up until it explodes. They might still have rocky moments, but they typically find ways to bounce back.

Cancers who embrace this hidden resilience often discover they can handle more challenges than they first believed. They learn to trust that their caring nature can be a source of strength, not a weakness. Realizing that tears or heartache can be part of healing helps them approach life's trials with courage.

Intuitive Decision-Making

Closely related to emotional awareness is Cancer's intuition. While logic and facts are important, Cancers also rely on gut feelings to guide them. Sometimes, they might sense something is off before any clear evidence appears. In friendships, they might spot a dishonest intention. In careers, they may realize a project is not on the right track even when everything looks normal on paper.

When balanced with practical thinking, this intuition can be a powerful tool. It can help them notice hidden risks or potential gains that others might overlook. For instance, a Cancer might pick the right moment to bring up a new idea at work because they sense their boss is in a receptive mood. Or they might avoid a risky venture because they feel it is not aligned with their personal values.

The more a Cancer refines this intuition—by paying attention to how it arises and learning from outcomes—the stronger it can become. They might keep a small record of times they followed a hunch and note whether it was correct. This self-awareness can strengthen their ability to make good decisions based on both feelings and facts.

Ability to Build Supportive Networks

Cancers are skilled at forging strong bonds. They know how to be good listeners, give empathetic advice, and stay true when someone needs them. This often leads to friendships or professional connections that last for many years. People enjoy the comfort and sincerity that Cancer brings, making them feel welcomed.

If they wish, Cancers can use this knack to create supportive groups. They might gather folks who share a common interest—like an art club or a charitable effort—to meet regularly, share insights, and form friendships. In a workplace, they could set up weekly lunches or short team-building events that help coworkers see each other as caring human beings, not just colleagues.

Over time, these networks can become a resource not just for Cancer, but for everyone involved. When someone needs help, the group responds. When good news comes, they share it together. This sense of community can be a major strength in times when people often feel disconnected or overlooked.

Deep Compassion for Causes and Issues

Beyond personal ties, Cancer can have a strong drive to help on a bigger scale. Seeing someone in need often moves them to act. Whether it is a neighborhood project or a global cause, they might feel called to pitch in with time, resources, or emotional support.

This compassion can turn into a meaningful part of their life. Some may volunteer at local shelters, gather supplies for families, or assist older people in the community. Others might focus on health or environmental issues, lending their empathy and organizational skills to campaigns or events.

Such efforts highlight Cancer's potential to make a difference. They can inspire others through sincere care, encouraging friends or coworkers to pitch in as well. Over time, they may become community leaders in their own right, recognized for their ability to bring warmth and practical help wherever it is needed.

Skill in Soothing Emotional Tension

When arguments or sadness arise, many people hesitate or say, "That's not my problem." Cancer, by contrast, often steps forward to calm the waters. They might talk privately with a friend who is upset, offering a hug or a kind word. Or they might suggest a peaceful compromise when two people disagree.

This ability to soothe tension can be very valuable in families, workplaces, and social groups. It prevents small problems from growing into major disputes. It also helps create an environment where people feel safe sharing concerns. Over time, Cancer might become the person everyone trusts to handle emotional ups and downs fairly.

Though this can be a big responsibility, it also shows that Cancer has a gift for emotional harmony. If they learn to set personal boundaries—so they do not carry everyone's burdens—they can keep using this skill without burning out. It is a clear strength that helps both them and those around them.

Practical Problem-Solving at Home

Though we often picture Cancer as emotional, they can also be quite practical, especially regarding home matters. They tend to notice if a space is cluttered, if bills are overdue, or if someone needs extra blankets. They have a watchful eye for small details that keep life running smoothly.

Because of this, they can excel in roles like homemaking, event planning, or property management if they choose to pursue them. They might also be the one in a friend group who arranges potluck lists, ensures that travel plans are set, or checks that everyone has a ride. This practical side complements their caring nature, allowing them to show love through action.

Cancers can push this skill further by learning organizational systems, budgeting approaches, or time management methods. With these methods, they can blend warmth with order, making sure the people they love (or work with) have what they need while keeping life tidy.

Personal Growth Through Shared Experiences

Cancer grows not just by personal introspection but by sharing life with others. They learn from how friends handle heartbreak, how a colleague deals with stress, or how a family member overcomes an obstacle. Because they watch emotions closely, they can gather lessons from each situation.

Then, they apply these insights to their own life. For example, they might notice a friend found comfort in painting during a tough time. Cancer could try that, discovering it helps with their own worries. Or they might see a coworker being assertive in meetings, inspiring them to speak up more.

This open-minded approach to learning shows how Cancer can tap into a world of possibilities. They do not have to face every challenge alone. By observing and engaging with others, they build a broader understanding, which then fuels their own potential to become well-rounded and confident.

Warmth That Motivates People

Sometimes, the greatest influence is not through sharp logic or stern commands but through warmth and encouragement. When Cancer believes in someone, that person often feels a surge of confidence. Words like "I know you can do this" or "I'm proud of your effort" can be life-changing in a moment of doubt.

This motivational style can be useful in any leadership role or personal relationship. A parent with a Cancer personality might consistently uplift a child's spirits, guiding them to discover their talents. A Cancer friend could gently push a hesitant peer to try a new hobby or apply for a scholarship.

Over time, this positivity helps Cancer become a source of quiet inspiration. People remember how they felt around Cancer—valued, supported, and braver than before. That sense of warmth can ripple out, encouraging a chain of kindness.

Flexibility in Adapting to Emotional Shifts

Although moods can change quickly for a Cancer, they also learn to adjust as needed. If they wake up feeling down, they might rearrange their schedule slightly to include a relaxing break. If a friend suddenly needs them, they often find time to listen and help. This adaptability can be a powerful asset.

In group settings, they can pivot when surprises happen. Perhaps a speaker cancels last minute, so Cancer suggests a different plan that still keeps things on track. Or if a project hits an unexpected roadblock, they calmly gather the team to brainstorm a fresh solution. This calm adjustment shows mental agility, which can make them reliable in any environment.

The key is to recognize this flexibility as a genuine strength, not just a reaction to strong feelings. By seeing how they can reshape plans smoothly, Cancers can feel proud of how resourceful they can be when life throws something unexpected their way.

Capacity for Lifelong Learning

Many Cancers remain open to learning new things well into adulthood. They might explore new recipes, study different art techniques, or pick up a skill like a foreign language. Their curiosity about people and the world leads them to keep growing and evolving.

If they set goals around personal development—such as taking short courses or joining book clubs—they can expand their minds without losing their strong sense of self. Their emotional intelligence pairs well with knowledge, allowing them to connect facts and data with human experiences.

This lifelong learning can also enhance their career paths. While they may not chase the highest titles, the skills and insights they gather can turn them into valuable team members or even entrepreneurs. Because they blend knowledge with empathy, they might find niche areas where they can thrive, such as counseling, teaching, or community leadership.

Skill at Creating Comfort in Tough Times

When tragedy or hardship hits, Cancer is often among the first to offer practical help. They might show up with cooked meals, comforting blankets, or a sincere ear for listening. This capacity to bring comfort in dark moments is one of their most heartwarming traits.

Families in need may find that Cancer organizes help, whether that is sending out messages to gather donations or quietly stepping in to handle everyday tasks. Friends facing loss might appreciate how Cancer takes the time to cry with them, reflecting empathy that is both gentle and genuine.

In a broader sense, this skill is a form of leadership, showing others how to respond with kindness when life gets hard. By using their instincts, Cancers can stand out as true supporters and can inspire others to do the same.

Thoughtful Decision-Making for Big Life Steps

Cancers generally do not rush into major life choices, like a big move or a marriage. They weigh the emotional impact, consider the effects on family or friends, and analyze how the decision aligns with their personal values. This careful approach may take time, but it often leads to well-considered outcomes.

By looking at both feelings and facts, they reduce the risk of rash moves that could harm themselves or others. They also bring in the perspectives of people who will be affected, gathering insights that might be overlooked by a more single-minded sign. While they might need to watch out for overthinking or fear of rejection, their thoroughness usually pays off in the form of stable, happier results.

Potential to Succeed in Service-Oriented Fields

When it comes to career possibilities, Cancers have a real edge in any field focused on care or service. Whether it is teaching, medical work, hospitality, counseling, or social advocacy, they can shine because of their natural desire to help. Their emotional intelligence can also be key in fields like human resources, therapy, or mediation, where understanding feelings is central to success.

Some might find fulfillment in running a small business that aligns with their sense of home, like a daycare or a cozy café. Others could excel in nonprofit roles, where empathy and loyalty drive them to push for change. The main point is that any role that allows a Cancer to show kindness and sincerity can become a place of thriving.

If they also bring a bit of business sense or organizational skill, they can turn these service-driven careers into stable and rewarding paths. They can build teams that reflect their supportive style, attracting clients or communities that appreciate a warm touch.

Personal Influence Through Storytelling and Media

Because Cancers are so tuned into feelings, they can be natural storytellers, whether through writing, film, or social media. By sharing personal experiences or emotional lessons, they can reach people's hearts. This influence can be used for good, spreading messages of understanding or highlighting important social concerns.

They might keep a personal blog that talks about daily ups and downs with honesty, touching readers who see their own experiences reflected. Or they could record music that captures the quiet struggles people go through, offering a sense of comfort. In a time when many feel isolated, a Cancer's candid approach can stand out as genuine and connecting.

If they want, they can grow this storytelling gift by studying writing, media production, or public speaking. The combination of strong empathy and clear expression can lead them to become strong voices in areas they care about.

Ability to Merge Tradition with Innovation

Cancers often appreciate traditions—keeping family recipes alive or preserving certain rituals—but they can also be open to fresh ideas. This blend lets them strike a balance between respecting the past and welcoming the new. In a practical sense, they might redesign an old family dish with healthier ingredients, or update a classic home layout with modern touches while still keeping the nostalgic feel.

At work, they may respect established methods while suggesting gentle improvements. This respectful approach can help them get support from both older colleagues who value tradition and younger ones who want to see progress. It is a unique skill: honoring what came before while not getting stuck in outdated ways.

Strong Sense of Purpose in Close Bonds

Finally, one of Cancer's biggest strengths is finding meaning in close connections. They see relationships not just as casual links but as roots that nourish their whole life. This strong sense of purpose can motivate them to work harder, grow personally, and face challenges with more determination.

When they form friendships or romantic bonds, they often bring a deep sense of devotion. They might plan small surprises, remember special dates, or spend hours comforting a loved one who is sad. In return, they usually receive a degree of loyalty that matches their own, creating a cycle of kindness and trust.

This feeling of purpose does not stop with personal ties. It can extend to coworkers, neighbors, or even strangers in need. By caring about people genuinely, Cancer finds a reason to keep trying, to keep improving, and to keep extending a helping hand. This core motivation fuels many of their best qualities, inspiring them to share warmth even when times are tough.

CHAPTER 12: HANDLING EMOTIONAL UPS AND DOWNS

Emotions run deep for Cancer, and along with that depth often comes shifts in mood. One day might feel steady and calm, the next day might bring tears or anxiety. These rises and falls are not flaws; they are part of having a sensitive mind and heart. Still, it can be exhausting or confusing to manage these swings, and it can also affect loved ones if they do not know how to respond.

This chapter focuses on practical methods that Cancer can use to handle emotional highs and lows. We will look at ways to recognize the start of a shift, what to do when feelings become overwhelming, and how to ensure these swings do not harm important relationships. Rather than fighting emotions, the goal is to find healthy ways to ride the waves, giving room for genuine feelings without being controlled by them.

Understanding the Roots of Mood Shifts

For many Cancers, mood changes can happen suddenly. Yet these changes rarely come from nowhere. They might be triggered by stress at work, an unkind comment from someone they value, lack of sleep, or even a small conflict that reminds them of an old hurt.

Recognizing possible triggers is a helpful first step. Keeping a simple mood journal for a few weeks can reveal patterns. For example, a Cancer might notice that being around negative people drains them, or that skipping breakfast leads to irritability by midday. By mapping out these patterns, they can plan ways to reduce or handle triggers more effectively.

There is also a natural side to these shifts. The Moon, which is linked to Cancer, moves through phases every month, and some people feel this affects their moods more than they realize. Even if they do not literally track the Moon's phase, being aware of monthly or weekly patterns can be useful.

Spotting Early Warning Signs

Before a mood fully changes, there are often small clues. For some Cancers, a sinking feeling in the stomach, tensing of the shoulders, or an urge to sigh might mean a low mood is coming. For others, an annoyed reaction to minor things—like a tapping sound—could hint that tension is building.

By catching these signals early, it becomes easier to do something to prevent a deeper slump. This could be taking a short walk, doing quick breathing exercises, or talking to a friend. If they wait too long, the mood might become so strong that it is much harder to manage.

By learning their own body's signs—like faster heartbeat, sudden tiredness, or restless thoughts—Cancers can create a "check-in" habit. When they notice one of these cues, they can pause, take a calming breath, and decide what will help most in that moment.

Healthy Outlets for Tough Emotions

When negative emotions rise, blocking or denying them often leads to more tension. Instead, it can help to let them out in a healthy way. This release does not mean yelling at friends or crying in the middle of a meeting. It is about having tools that allow feelings to exit without causing harm.

Some simple outlets include:

- **Journaling**: Writing down worries or anger can bring relief. It does not need to be neat or organized—just a brain-dump of emotions.

- **Art**: Sketching, coloring, or painting can channel feelings into a visual form. Even simple doodles can help.

- **Music**: Listening to songs that match the mood can be a form of release. If they play an instrument, letting out feelings in a melody can be calming.

- **Physical Activity**: Taking a brisk walk, dancing, or doing easy stretches can help burn off stress hormones.

By keeping these outlets ready, Cancer can use them as soon as they feel the negative mood getting stronger. This prevents a buildup of unspoken feelings that might later come out as tears or sharp words.

Talking to Supportive People

Having a trusted friend or family member to confide in can make a big difference during emotional lows. Cancers often feel better just by sharing what is on their mind. A friend's calm statement—like "I hear you, and it sounds tough"—can bring huge comfort.

However, it is important to choose the right person. Some people are uncomfortable with deep feelings or might respond with impatience. A Cancer should look for someone who listens without judgment or tries to "fix" everything too quickly. If no such person is available, talking to a counselor or therapist can be a safe option.

When sharing, it helps to be honest about what they need. If they just want to vent, they can say, "I just need to get this off my chest. I'm not looking for advice right now." This removes pressure from both sides and reduces the chance of feeling misunderstood.

Dealing with Anxiety

For some Cancers, emotional swings include waves of worry or anxiety. They might sense their heart racing, muscles tightening, and thoughts racing in circles. When anxiety hits, it can be easy to feel stuck.

Short techniques can help:

- **Deep Breathing**: Inhale slowly for a count of four, hold for four, then exhale for four. Repeating this helps the body shift into a calmer state.

- **Grounding Exercises**: Name five things around the room, four sounds, three textures, two smells, and one taste. This anchors the mind in the present.

- **Positive Reminders**: Replacing frantic thoughts with gentler ones like, "I can handle this moment," can ease panic.

If anxiety is a frequent visitor, more structured help might be wise—like brief therapy sessions that teach coping methods or journaling each day to track triggers. Over time, these steps can keep anxiety from derailing a Cancer's emotional balance.

Handling Sudden Upswings

Emotional highs can be wonderful, filling Cancer with excitement or joy, but they can also lead to impulsive actions if not handled with care. Sometimes, a sudden feeling of euphoria might cause them to overspend, promise too much, or ignore important tasks.

While it is good to enjoy bright moods, it helps to keep some common-sense limits. For instance, if they feel a strong urge to buy gifts for everyone, they can pause to review their budget. If they want to throw a large party on a whim, they might check with a friend for a second opinion.

Upswings can also be harnessed. If they feel energetic, they might tackle a creative project or plan a small social event that fits their schedule. By channeling that happy energy into productive or fun activities, they make the most of these positive stretches without setting themselves up for problems when the feeling cools off.

Communicating Mood Changes with Loved Ones

People around Cancer might not always know when a mood swing is happening, especially if outward signs are subtle. This can lead to misunderstandings, as a partner or friend might take Cancer's quiet or abrupt tone as personal rejection.

A simple solution is to give a gentle heads-up: "I'm feeling a bit off today, so if I seem distant, it's not about you." This short statement can save a lot of confusion. Loved ones then understand that Cancer is going through an internal shift, not suddenly upset with them.

Sharing specific requests can help, too. They might say, "I might need some space to clear my head," or "I'd love a hug if that's okay."

This clarity allows friends or family to respond in supportive ways without guessing.

Self-Care Rituals for Stability

Building small self-care steps into each day can keep mood swings from being overwhelming. A brief morning routine, like taking a few deep breaths by an open window, or sipping a soothing drink while quietly thinking, can set a steady tone for the day.

In the evening, winding down with soft music or writing three good things that happened can help them process any leftover tension. On weekends, they might schedule a bit of alone time to recharge, even if it is just an hour of reading or a calm walk.

These rituals do not have to be elaborate or time-consuming. The key is consistency. By making them part of daily life, Cancer ensures that emotional balance is actively maintained, reducing sudden dips or spikes.

Knowing When to Seek Professional Help

While many mood swings are within normal limits, there are times when a Cancer might realize their emotional ups and downs are too strong or last too long. If sadness or anxiety interferes with work, relationships, or basic self-care, it might be wise to seek professional help.

Therapists, counselors, or support groups can offer tools suited to a person's specific situation. There is no shame in reaching out for such assistance; it can be a step toward greater stability and well-being. Sometimes, medication is also an option if a qualified professional thinks it is needed.

The key is noticing if mood swings become so intense that daily functioning is a struggle. Early action can prevent deeper problems and teach healthy patterns that benefit Cancer for years to come.

Handling Anger in a Controlled Way

It is not unusual for Cancer, who tends to avoid conflict, to let small irritations build up until they explode. This can turn into an outburst of anger that surprises everyone. Learning to vent anger in controlled ways prevents damage to relationships or self-esteem.

They can:

- **Address Problems Early**: Speak up when upset, instead of letting anger brew.

- **Use Physical Outlets**: Punching a pillow, squeezing a stress ball, or doing an active chore can release pent-up energy.

- **Cool Down Before Talking**: If anger is hot, taking a few minutes to step away and breathe can stop hurtful words.

By handling anger in a healthier manner, Cancer can stay true to their caring nature without bottling up negative feelings. It is not about never feeling mad, but rather about expressing it in ways that cause the least harm and bring the most relief.

Protecting Against Emotional Overload

Because Cancer is sensitive, they may pick up on other people's stress or sadness. If they spend a day comforting multiple friends, they might end up carrying a heavy emotional load. This can lead to burnout or an unexpected crash.

To guard against overload, they can learn to set personal limits. For example, if a friend wants to talk late at night about drama, Cancer might say, "I want to be there for you, but I need to rest soon. Can we talk tomorrow?" They might also schedule quiet hours after big social events, giving themselves room to decompress.

When they realize they have taken on too much, it is okay to step back and recharge. That might mean turning off the phone for an evening, taking a calming bath, or simply lying down and letting the mind wander freely.

Using Positive Affirmations

Sometimes, mood dips come from negative self-talk: "I'm not good enough," "I always mess up," or "No one really cares." Replacing these thoughts with kinder statements can create a more balanced mindset.

Examples of gentle self-talk include:

- "I might have flaws, but I also have good qualities."

- "I can handle this situation step by step."

- "I am worthy of love and support."

Repeating such statements when bad thoughts arise can slowly shift the mind's default setting. Over time, these affirmations may become natural, reducing the intensity of negative swings.

Dealing with Emotional Whiplash

Sometimes, a Cancer might swing from a happy high to a sad low in a short span, leaving them feeling like they are on an emotional roller coaster. This whiplash can be tiring. One strategy is to pause and ask, "What triggered this sudden flip?" Maybe it was a piece of news or a remembered worry.

If the cause is something small, recognizing it might help them return to a stable place quickly. If it is something big, they can plan a response. For instance, if a text from an ex-partner triggered sadness, they could choose to put the phone aside or talk it through with a friend. Identifying the trigger gives them some control over the next step.

Working with Relaxation Methods

To manage strong moods, many Cancers find value in relaxation methods. These might include:

Meditation: Sitting quietly and focusing on the breath.

Gentle Yoga: Pairing stretches with mindful breathing.

Nature Walks: Observing trees, birds, or water can calm the mind.

Progressive Muscle Relaxation: Tensing and relaxing muscle groups from head to toe.

Practicing these methods even when feeling okay can build a stronger base, so when big waves of emotion arrive, the mind is better prepared to stay calm.

Creating a Peaceful Living Space

Since Cancer usually finds comfort in a cozy home, adjusting the living space to be more calming can make a difference in emotional health. This could mean choosing soft colors, adding comforting textures (like thick blankets or plush rugs), and placing photos or items that bring happy memories in view.

Soft lighting rather than harsh overhead lights can also help. Some Cancers enjoy salt lamps or string lights that emit a gentle glow. A few houseplants might bring a soothing touch of nature indoors. The aim is to create a sanctuary that supports emotional regulation.

Building a Mood Toolkit

Because emotional swings are likely, it can help to keep a "mood toolkit." This is a small collection of items or activities that quickly bring comfort or distract from negative states. It might include:

- A playlist of uplifting or calming songs
- A small book of inspiring quotes
- A coloring book and markers
- A favorite snack
- A few scented oils or lotions

When a tough mood hits, they can reach for something in this toolkit. Even a few minutes of coloring while listening to gentle music can shift the mood enough to think more clearly.

Scheduling Downtime

Sometimes, a busy life does not leave much room for emotional resets. Cancers might find themselves rushing from work to family tasks, with no gap to breathe. Planning a small block of downtime each day, or at least a few times a week, can help.

Downtime could be as simple as sitting alone for 15 minutes with no screens and just letting thoughts settle. Or it might be a calming hobby like knitting or assembling puzzles. The point is to remove the rush and let feelings settle into a quieter place, preventing emotional overload.

Telling a Loved One How to Help

Friends and family might want to help but not know what to do when Cancer's mood changes. A direct conversation can help. Cancer could say, "When I get anxious, it helps if someone calmly talks me through it. But I don't like it when people raise their voices or tell me I'm overreacting."

By sharing specific do's and don'ts, they teach others the best ways to show support. Most loved ones are glad to have clear instructions rather than guessing. This also avoids the frustration of well-meaning attempts that do not match Cancer's needs.

Keeping Perspective During Highs and Lows

When emotions run high—whether joy or sadness—it is easy to believe this feeling will last forever. But in reality, moods are temporary. Reminding themselves that "This will pass" can bring a sense of calm.

If they are extremely happy, they might note, "I should enjoy this, but remember things will feel normal again soon." If they are very sad, they can remind themselves, "This is painful, but I've felt better before and will feel better again." This simple idea often prevents acting on fleeting emotions in ways that cause regret later.

Reflection and Lessons Learned

After a mood swing passes, it can be helpful to look back and ask, "What happened here?" Maybe they learned a new trigger or found a coping method that worked well. Keeping track of these lessons in a notebook or mental log helps them handle similar situations better next time.

Over months or years, this reflection leads to self-growth. Each emotional wave becomes a chance to gather insights, making the next wave easier to ride. This is how sensitivity can turn into wisdom, with Cancer gaining deeper knowledge about their own emotional landscape.

Sharing Creative Expressions with Others

Sometimes, dealing with emotions is easier if a Cancer shares the outcome of their creative expressions. For example, if they write a poem when sad, they might show it to a trusted friend. This can lead to support, feedback, or simply a sense of connection.

Other times, they might post their art or stories online in safe communities where people understand emotional depth. Receiving encouragement can reduce the isolation that often comes with mood swings. It reminds Cancer that their feelings can be used for art, bonding, or even helping others through similar troubles.

Avoiding Shame Around Emotions

Some cultures or families treat strong emotions as something to hide. Cancer might grow up thinking tears or vulnerability are signs of weakness. This shame can intensify mood swings, because they feel bad for having normal human reactions.

Rejecting this shame is a key step. Emotions are not shameful; they are part of being alive. Cancers can remind themselves that their sensitivity is a gift that allows them to empathize, create, and love deeply. If anyone criticizes them for "feeling too much," they can choose to stand firm, knowing that emotional expression is healthy when handled responsibly.

Seeking a Balance Between Solitude and Connection

When a mood swing hits, Cancer might either crave being alone or crave company. Finding a balance is crucial. If they isolate for too long, they might sink further into sadness. If they force themselves to be around people when they need space, they might grow irritable.

By listening to their instincts, they can decide which is best at the moment. A quick text to a close friend might help them feel less alone, followed by some private rest. Or if they have been alone too much, they might invite a friend for a short walk or coffee chat. Balancing these needs reduces mood extremes.

Handling Emotional Swings in the Workplace

It can be tricky to handle ups and downs at work, where professionalism is expected. If a low mood strikes at the office, a Cancer could take a brief break—maybe a bathroom visit to do a breathing exercise or a slow walk around the block. They might also confide quietly in a sympathetic coworker, explaining they need a moment before diving back into tasks.

If a high mood is distracting, they can channel that energy into tasks that require excitement or creativity. If the workplace environment is strict, they might jot down ideas in a notebook to explore later, keeping focus on priority tasks until break time.

Encouraging a Supportive Circle

Friends or family who understand Cancer's emotional style can make a huge difference. That might mean explaining to a friend group why certain topics or environments trigger sadness, or calmly telling siblings how to respond when Cancer becomes anxious. Over time, this creates a circle of support where everyone respects each other's emotional needs.

Such a circle can also offer perspective. If Cancer worries about something minor, a trusted friend might gently say, "I think you might be overreacting. Let's talk it through." Because there is a foundation of trust, Cancer can listen without feeling attacked.

Preventing Guilt Over Mood Changes

Sometimes, Cancer feels guilty if their mood swings inconvenience others. They might think, "I'm a burden," or "I'm ruining the fun." But guilt only adds another layer of negative feeling.

A kinder view is that everyone has moods, and it is okay to have an off day. Apologizing if they snapped at someone can be enough to smooth things over. They do not need to apologize for simply being sad or worried. True friends and family understand that emotions are part of being human.

Combining Logic with Emotion

One method to handle swings is to bring a bit of logical thinking when feelings become too strong. For instance, if Cancer feels a sudden fear that a friend secretly dislikes them, they can ask, "What evidence do I have for this?" Maybe the friend has always been kind, and the fear is just an anxious thought.

Balancing emotion with reason can prevent negative assumptions from spiraling. Writing a short pros and cons list for a situation can help ground them in reality. This does not remove feelings, but it puts them in context, allowing for clearer decisions.

Long-Term Stability Strategies

Over the years, as Cancer learns about their emotional waves, they can build a stable foundation. This might involve:

Consistent Sleep: Going to bed and waking up at regular times to keep the body rested.

Nutritious Eating: Avoiding blood sugar spikes that can worsen mood swings.

Exercise: Gentle physical activity that releases endorphins and lowers stress.

Planned Relaxation: Booking short vacations or quiet weekends regularly, not just when at breaking point.

These habits create a smoother day-to-day existence, reducing the intensity of swings and helping Cancer stay balanced.

Conclusion

Emotional ups and downs are part of life for many Cancers, reflecting a deep sensitivity that can be both a blessing and a challenge. By learning to spot triggers early, build healthy outlets, communicate needs, and practice self-care, they can move through these shifts without losing themselves. Rather than seeing mood swings as a flaw, they can treat them as signals that the heart is alive and responding strongly to the world.

With careful attention, they can keep their emotional waters from flooding their days. Solid support from friends, self-awareness about triggers, and gentle acceptance of their feelings can all combine to form a strong foundation. This foundation allows them to share their caring spirit with others while still protecting their own well-being. Over time, a Cancer can harness these waves into a rhythm of life that honors sensitivity yet remains balanced, steady, and nurturing.

CHAPTER 13: RELAXATION AND SELF-CARE

Cancer is a sign that often feels things deeply, noticing small changes in mood or environment. This depth brings many strengths, like empathy and creativity, but it can also lead to stress if left unchecked. Relaxation and self-care become vital for Cancer to stay balanced. In this chapter, we will explore how to form habits of rest and renewal. We will look at new techniques that fit Cancer's sensitive nature, covering physical, mental, and emotional practices. We will also discuss tips for creating a soothing environment, plus ideas for self-care that go beyond the basics.

Why Relaxation and Self-Care Matter for Cancer

For many Cancers, emotions can pile up quickly. Caring for friends, family, or coworkers can be draining if they never take time for themselves. Over time, stress might show up as sleep troubles, headaches, or a short temper. Relaxation and self-care are not just luxuries; they protect overall health.

When well-rested and calm, a Cancer can express their empathy without feeling overwhelmed. They can be present with loved ones, make clear decisions, and find happiness in the small events of life. Lack of rest and personal care, on the other hand, can lead to emotional overload that affects relationships and day-to-day activities.

Relaxation also helps Cancer tap into their creative side. When the mind is at ease, new ideas or artistic inspiration can bubble up naturally. Even a short break can refresh their outlook, allowing them to return to tasks with fresh energy.

Defining Self-Care in a Personal Way

People often think self-care means spa trips or fancy baths. While these can help, self-care for Cancer involves any activity that nourishes the mind or body. It might be a few quiet minutes in the morning, a comforting hobby after work, or chatting with a friend who offers genuine support.

The point is to choose actions that truly soothe the soul. A Cancer who loves home life might find peace in rearranging a bedroom to feel cozier. Another person might prefer strolling through a park to get fresh air. One size does not fit all, so it is good to explore different methods until finding the ones that resonate most deeply.

Self-care can also be very simple. Even pausing to watch clouds for a few minutes can bring a sense of calm if done with focus. The key is consistency. Short daily breaks tend to be more effective in the long run than occasional big efforts.

Gentle Daily Routines

Since Cancer values security, having small daily routines can be comforting. A consistent wake-up and bedtime schedule is one example. Waking up at the same time each day helps regulate the body's internal clock, leading to better sleep and steadier energy levels.

In the morning, a Cancer might do a quick stretch or sip a warm drink while thinking of a positive intention for the day. This moment of calm provides a gentle start. Even if the rest of the day is full of tasks, that small pocket of peace can anchor the mind.

In the evening, winding down with soft lighting, minimal screen time, and quiet music can signal the body that it is time to rest. Over time, these routines become like comforting rituals that protect mental space from the demands of the outside world.

Body-Friendly Relaxation

Relaxation for Cancer often involves soothing physical tension. When the body is tight, the mind can become restless. Some methods that help release tension include:

Progressive Muscle Relaxation: Lie or sit down in a comfortable spot. Start at the toes, gently tensing and then releasing each group of muscles upward through the body. This simple sequence can calm both muscles and mind.

Gentle Yoga or Stretching: Slow stretching, especially in the neck, shoulders, and back, can ease typical tension areas. A short practice in the morning or before bed can do wonders for stress relief.

Warm Baths or Foot Soaks: Water is often linked to the Cancer sign. Soaking in warm water can ease tightness, and adding mild scents like lavender or chamomile may boost relaxation. Even if a full bath is not possible, soaking the feet in a basin of warm water can feel just as soothing.

Light Massage or Self-Massage: Pressing gently on tense areas, such as the shoulders or lower back, can promote blood flow and help the body feel more open. Some Cancers like to use a roller ball or massaging device if they do not have a partner or friend to help.

Moving the body in gentle ways helps free up energy that might be locked in stress. Each of these practices can be adapted to the time and space available. Even a few minutes can make a significant difference if done regularly.

Mindful Breathing for Quick Calm

Breathing is often overlooked as a self-care tool, but it can shift the body and mind into a calmer state very quickly. When stress hits, the breath tends to become shallow or fast. By taking deliberate slow breaths, a Cancer can signal to the nervous system that it is okay to relax.

One simple method is **Box Breathing**:

1. Inhale for a count of four.

2. Hold for a count of four.

3. Exhale for a count of four.

4. Pause again for a count of four.

Repeat several times. This pattern steadies the breath and can be done almost anywhere—at a desk, in a car (while parked), or even standing in line. When tension creeps in, just a minute of box breathing can reset the mood.

Another approach is **5-5-5-5 breathing**: Inhale for five seconds, hold for five, exhale for five, hold again for five, then repeat. It is similar but extends the time slightly, which some might find more comforting.

Balancing Alone Time and Social Time

Cancers often enjoy being around people they care about, yet they also have a strong need for quiet moments. Finding the right balance of alone time and social time is key to self-care. If they isolate for too long, they might feel lonely. If they spend too much time in big groups, they can become overwhelmed.

A good practice is to plan social events with breaks in between. For instance, if a family gathering happens on Saturday, they might keep Sunday more open for rest. If a Cancer sees that their week is packed with plans every evening, they might block out one evening as quiet time to recharge.

During alone time, they can do soothing activities—reading a comforting book, tidying a corner of the house to feel more at ease, or even napping if needed. By listening to their emotional cues, they can sense when it is time to retreat and when it is time to connect.

Creative Outlets for Stress Relief

In a previous chapter, we touched on creativity as a strength for Cancer, but it also serves as a potent self-care tool. Activities like drawing, journaling, knitting, or music-making can allow the mind to drift into a peaceful focus. When a Cancer immerses themselves in a creative act, worries often fade into the background.

It is important to choose a creative outlet that feels fun rather than forced. If painting is too messy, they might try coloring books or digital art apps. If playing music seems too involved, simple humming along to a favorite tune can still release emotional tension. The key is letting the process, not the final product, bring relaxation.

Some Cancers enjoy cooking or baking as a creative release. Trying new recipes can be both satisfying and soothing if done at a leisurely pace. They might put on calm music, measure ingredients carefully, and focus on the textures, smells, and tastes. This mindful approach turns a basic chore into a form of self-care.

Nature as a Healing Space

Many Cancers feel drawn to water, but any natural setting can help them unwind. Spending time outdoors—whether at a beach, near a lake, or in a local park—can refresh the mind. Listening to birds, feeling a breeze, or watching water flow can all calm racing thoughts.

Even in a city, small pockets of green can be found. A Cancer might seek out a community garden or a quiet bench under a tree. If stepping outside is difficult, bringing nature indoors can help. Keeping houseplants or a small herb garden in the kitchen can offer a soothing vibe.

Outdoor walks provide gentle exercise and fresh air. For a Cancer who works indoors, a short walk during lunch break might turn a hectic day into a more bearable one. Observing small details—like leaves on the ground or patterns in the clouds—helps shift focus away from stress.

Building a Cozy Environment

The physical space a Cancer inhabits can greatly affect how they feel. Messy or chaotic surroundings might heighten anxiety, while a comfortable, tidy space can support calm. They do not have to aim for a perfect home, but having a cozy corner or room helps with relaxation.

Choosing soothing colors like soft blues, gentle greys, or warm neutrals can make a difference. Adding plush blankets, comfortable pillows, and gentle lighting creates a haven where stress tends to fade. Some Cancers like to include sentimental items—photos, shells from a special beach, or gifts from loved ones—to enhance the sense of emotional safety.

Scent can also play a part. Mild aromas—such as lavender, rose, chamomile, or sandalwood—might be used in diffusers or candles to set a calm mood. If scents are too strong, natural fresh air from an open window can be just as good. The main idea is to make the home environment an ally in self-care rather than a source of clutter or stress.

Digital Boundaries

Modern life often brings many digital distractions. Constant phone alerts, social media updates, and news feeds can feed into a Cancer's natural sensitivity, causing them to absorb more information (and stress) than they can handle. Setting digital boundaries is a powerful form of self-care.

This might mean turning off unnecessary notifications, especially during evening hours when the mind needs to settle. Some Cancers choose to keep their phone in a different room at night, preventing the glow of screens from interfering with sleep.

Social media can also trigger comparisons or negativity if used without caution. A Cancer might limit daily browsing time or unfollow accounts that bring unwanted stress. Curating a feed that uplifts rather than drains can keep them from slipping into anxious states.

The Power of Relaxing Rituals

Rituals are different from simple habits. They have an intentional quality that can bring deep calm. A relaxing ritual could be as small as lighting a candle every evening and spending five minutes reflecting on the day. It could be sipping tea while watching the sunrise.

For Cancer, linking these rituals to water can be extra soothing. A nightly foot soak, for instance, or running a humidifier with a mild aroma can act as a reminder to let go of the day's weight. Even washing dishes by hand can become a gentle ritual if done slowly and mindfully, feeling the water temperature and focusing on the repetitive motions.

The purpose is not the act itself but the sense of comfort and intention behind it. Over time, these rituals become anchors, signaling to the mind that it is time to relax and release tension.

Listening to the Body's Signals

Cancers can sometimes ignore physical signs like fatigue or small aches if they are busy helping others. Self-care means tuning in to the body's whispers. If they notice back discomfort from sitting too long, a quick stretch might prevent bigger pain later. If they feel unusually tired, it could be a sign to rest earlier or lighten the schedule.

Similarly, changes in appetite, headaches, or persistent restlessness can be clues that emotional stress is building. A Cancer who pays attention to these signals can address issues before they grow into bigger problems. Whether that means taking a mental health day, speaking with a professional, or just catching a nap, responding early can save a lot of distress.

Embracing Calm Hobbies

Self-care often becomes easier if woven into hobbies that foster calm. A Cancer might find enjoyment in activities like puzzle-solving, calligraphy, or gentle gardening. These are hobbies that do not push for competition or high stakes but allow for pleasant engagement of the mind.

Puzzle-solving can be a metaphor for organizing thoughts. As they put pieces together, they may notice their mind feels more organized too. Calligraphy or handwriting practice demands slow, graceful movements, which can steady scattered thinking. Gardening connects them to nature's rhythms, teaching patience and offering small rewards like fresh herbs or flowers.

By choosing calm hobbies, Cancer can have a built-in self-care practice that also feels like leisure. It is not about performance but about experiencing the soothing process.

Self-Compassion vs. Self-Criticism

Cancers sometimes lean toward self-criticism, especially if they feel they have let someone down. This can undo efforts to relax, since negative thoughts may creep in during quiet moments. Learning self-compassion is crucial.

Self-compassion involves talking to oneself kindly instead of harshly. If something goes wrong, a Cancer can say, "I tried my best. I can learn from this, but it does not define my worth." This mental shift helps them relax more fully, free from the inner voice that might otherwise list every flaw or mistake.

They might also practice short self-compassion breaks, placing a hand on their heart and reminding themselves that mistakes are part of being human. Over time, these small gestures strengthen emotional resilience, making it easier to bounce back from stress.

Setting Boundaries as Self-Care

Saying "no" to extra responsibilities, especially when already feeling stretched, is an act of self-care. Cancers often want to help, but they risk burnout if they take on too many tasks. Boundaries protect mental energy and ensure they can give genuine care rather than forced effort.

A boundary could be refusing an invite when exhausted, politely explaining, "I'm sorry, but I need to rest tonight." It could be telling a coworker that another project cannot be done until next week, rather than rushing and feeling overwhelmed. Setting these limits might feel uncomfortable at first, but it pays off by preserving emotional health.

If guilt arises, a Cancer can remind themselves that others deserve a version of them that is present and well, not tired and resentful. Healthy boundaries do not mean they stop caring; they mean care is shared with self-protection in mind.

Trying Relaxation Apps or Tools

Today, many apps offer guided relaxation or meditation. Some have calming music, gentle instructions for breathing, or short visualizations. This can be handy for a Cancer who struggles to quiet the mind on their own. A quick session during a break might reset the mood in under ten minutes.

Physical tools like stress balls, fidget spinners, or handheld massagers can also help. They provide a simple outlet for restless energy. Some Cancers enjoy weighted blankets, which create a sense of gentle pressure that can soothe anxiety and improve sleep.

While these tools are not necessities, they can add variety to a self-care routine. The key is to use them with intention—focusing on the act rather than rushing through it. This mindful use of apps or tools can bring an immediate sense of relief.

Encouraging Self-Care in Group Settings

Sometimes, self-care is easier when shared. A Cancer could plan a quiet evening with a friend, each doing their own relaxing activity together. Or they might form a small "self-care circle" where members meet once a week to unwind.

Group yoga sessions, guided meditations, or nature walks are all ways to combine companionship with calmness. This approach can motivate a Cancer who struggles to keep up with self-care alone. When others join, it feels like a supportive gathering rather than a solo task that is easily postponed.

In families, setting a calm hour before bedtime for everyone can help the entire household. Perhaps no loud screens or arguments during that time—just reading, quiet crafts, or peaceful conversation. By making it a shared routine, each person supports the others' need for rest.

Reflecting on Good Moments

For a Cancer whose mind naturally notices what is wrong or who needs help, taking a moment each day to reflect on what went right can shift the mood. This is sometimes called a gratitude practice, but it can be as simple as listing three pleasant things that happened.

They might note small details: "I had a tasty breakfast," "The weather was nice," or "I laughed at a funny comment from a coworker." These might sound minor, but over time, noticing good moments can balance a tendency to focus on problems. It also trains the mind to see positive threads in daily life.

This reflection does not have to be written down, though journaling is an option. Even thinking through the positives while brushing teeth can set a calmer tone for bedtime. By ending the day with a short recollection of good moments, a Cancer can fall asleep feeling a bit lighter.

Accepting Help from Others

Self-care is sometimes about letting others step in. If a Cancer is consistently giving to friends or family, they might resist accepting help, worried about being a burden. Yet being open to support can lighten emotional loads.

This might mean saying yes when a friend offers to pick up groceries or babysit for a while. It could mean agreeing to a heartfelt talk when a loved one notices they are upset. Allowing help teaches Cancer that they do not have to carry everything alone. In fact, it can deepen bonds because friends or family feel trusted and valued.

If guilt arises, they can recall that people often feel good when their help is accepted. By letting others give back, Cancer fosters mutual care rather than a one-sided pattern. Over time, this balanced exchange reduces stress and strengthens relationships.

Handling Emotional Relapses

No matter how well a Cancer plans for self-care, there will be days when stress piles up or emotions run high. It is vital to remember that this does not mean they have failed at self-care. Ups and downs are normal.

When setbacks happen—such as a rough night's sleep or an argument with a close friend—returning to basic self-care steps can help them realign. Maybe that means a warm bath, an early bedtime, or a chat with a supportive person. These actions do not eliminate problems, but they provide the steady ground needed to face them.

Over time, each relapse can become part of a growing understanding of what works best. Some triggers might require more direct action, like seeking counseling or changing a stressful job. Others might be solved by simple rest and kindness to oneself.

Creating a Personal Self-Care "Menu"

Sometimes, deciding what to do for relaxation can feel daunting. A written "menu" of calming activities can make it easier. A Cancer can list actions that help, grouped by how much time or effort they take. For example:

Five-Minute Options

- Deep breathing exercise
- Quick stretch
- Sip water mindfully

- Look at a calming photo

Fifteen-Minute Options

- Short walk outside

- Brew tea and watch the steam

- Put on mellow music and rest eyes

- Write a quick reflection in a notebook

Longer Options

- Warm bath with soft lighting

- Paint or draw for half an hour

- Watch a comforting show or documentary

- Cook a simple meal with fresh ingredients

When feeling stressed, a Cancer can look at this menu and pick something that fits their mood and time. It removes the guesswork and encourages them to actually follow through on self-care rather than telling themselves, "I'll do something later."

Balancing Physical Health

Relaxation includes more than emotional well-being; physical health matters too. Getting enough sleep, eating nourishing food, and staying hydrated are foundational. If these basics slide, it is hard to feel calm.

Cancers can pay attention to how certain foods affect their mood. Some might find sugary snacks cause quick highs and then crashes, fueling emotional swings. Others might notice that a heavy meal before bed disrupts sleep. By making small adjustments—like choosing lighter evening meals or adding more vegetables—they might see smoother energy levels.

Regular medical check-ups also count as self-care. Catching potential issues early can prevent stress down the road. Knowing they are taking proactive steps for physical health can free the mind from worry.

Finding Supportive Communities

Support can come not only from close friends and family but also from communities where people share common interests or concerns. This could be an online group focused on anxiety tips, a local club for crafters, or a walking meetup.

Joining such communities allows Cancer to relax among like-minded individuals. They might learn new self-care ideas, discover local resources (like yoga studios or parks), or simply feel less isolated. The key is choosing communities that encourage kindness and understanding rather than competition or negative talk.

Scheduling "Nothing Time"

Though it sounds odd, one helpful self-care practice is scheduling a small block of time to do absolutely nothing. This is different from napping or reading. It means sitting or lying down without an agenda—no phone, no plan, just being.

For a sign that experiences strong inner feelings, this might be challenging at first. The mind might wander, or restlessness could creep in. But with practice, these short "nothing" sessions can lead to insights or a sense of deep calm. It is like giving the mind a chance to rest from constant stimulation.

Even five minutes a day can have benefits. Over time, some Cancers might extend it to ten or fifteen minutes if they find it helpful. The aim is not to force quiet but to allow whatever arises in the mind to pass by gently, kind of like watching clouds drift across the sky.

Encouraging Fun and Lightness

Sometimes, self-care is mistaken for only calm or serious activities. Fun and laughter are also forms of relaxation. A Cancer might watch a playful movie, try a silly game with friends, or engage in easy banter that lightens the mood.

Humor can cut through tension. Sharing a few funny moments or comedic videos with a friend might lift spirits quickly. The trick is to find humor that does not offend or create more stress. Gentle, upbeat humor suits a Cancer's caring nature, letting them laugh without guilt or worry.

Tracking Progress Without Stress

It can be motivating to see how self-care improves well-being over time. But for Cancers who dislike strict rules, a formal checklist might feel burdensome. A gentle approach could be keeping a small calendar and placing a sticker or a mark on days when they took some self-care action.

Over weeks, seeing these marks can inspire them to keep going. If they notice a stretch of days with no marks, they might realize they have let self-care slip. Then they can plan to add a break or schedule a relaxing activity. This helps them stay mindful of nurturing themselves.

Listening to Subtle Shifts

Sensitivity can be a strength here. Cancers might notice small changes in their stress level, emotions, or body aches sooner than others. By paying attention, they can respond with self-care before issues escalate.

For example, if the shoulders tense up during a tense conversation, they can pause for a quick shoulder roll or breathing break. If a headache starts in the afternoon, they can ask themselves if they drank enough water or took a break from the screen. These micro-adjustments prevent bigger meltdowns later on.

Self-Care During Busy Phases

Life sometimes gets busy, leaving little room for extensive self-care routines. Cancers can adapt by focusing on micro-practices:

- Stretch for 20 seconds every hour.

- Drink water regularly.

- Pause to take a slow breath between tasks.

- Step outside for a moment of fresh air, even if it is just on a balcony.

Small efforts matter. Five seconds of calm repeated multiple times a day can add up to a smoother emotional state. Once the busy period ends, they might plan a lengthier relaxation session, like a weekend break or a creative project.

Concluding Thoughts

For Cancer, self-care is not a one-time fix but an ongoing way of life. Emotions ebb and flow, stress can creep in from many directions, and personal needs change with time. By viewing relaxation as an essential practice, they can maintain a steadier sense of well-being, tapping into their natural warmth without burning out.

Whether it is a few minutes of deep breathing, a cozy bath at the end of a rough day, or a creative hobby that soothes the heart, self-care offers Cancer the chance to remain nurturing without losing themselves. It protects their kind spirit, strengthens resilience, and opens space for the gentle joys that make life meaningful.

CHAPTER 14: SPIRITUAL AND MYSTICAL THOUGHTS

Cancer, known for depth of feeling, often has a natural draw toward spiritual or mystical ideas. This does not mean every Cancer believes in cosmic forces, but many of them sense there is more to life than what meets the eye. They may find comfort or guidance in spiritual practices, folklore, or symbolic items that connect them to something bigger.

In this chapter, we explore how Cancer might view spiritual or mystical concepts. We look at how they might relate to the Moon and natural cycles, the roles of symbols and rituals, and ways they integrate spiritual beliefs into daily life. While no single path fits all, we will examine themes that resonate with Cancer's emotional and intuitive nature.

The Sign's Connection to the Moon

Cancer is traditionally linked to the Moon. Some believe this creates a closer bond between the sign and the lunar cycles. From new moon to full moon and back, many Cancers feel their moods mirror these changing phases.

Those who follow lunar cycles might do small rituals or reflections during different moon phases. For instance, they might use the new moon to quietly set fresh intentions or the full moon to reflect on recent progress and release lingering worries. These actions can be as simple as writing a short note about a goal or concern, then placing it somewhere safe.

Even if a Cancer does not follow strict lunar events, simply observing the moon in the sky can bring calm. Gazing at its changing shape can be a gentle reminder that everything shifts, including emotions. That knowledge can soothe them during low moods, knowing a brighter phase might be around the corner—just like the Moon returning to fullness.

Intuition and Inner Knowings

Cancers often trust their instincts, sensing undercurrents in relationships or environments that others miss. They might walk into a room and feel an immediate sense that something is off, or meet someone and quickly sense the person's emotional state. This heightened perception can lead them to explore spiritual ideas about energy, synchronicity, or psychic awareness.

Some might keep a small journal to track intuitive hunches. Writing down a guess about a situation, then later checking if it was correct, can sharpen this sixth sense. While not all instincts prove accurate, the process can help Cancers tune into subtle signals and find patterns in daily life.

Others might explore practices like tarot reading or oracle cards, seeing them as tools to spark intuition rather than predict the future. They might shuffle the cards, pull one, and reflect on how its themes connect to their current concerns. This reflection process can reveal hidden feelings or angles they had not considered.

Rituals for Emotional Cleansing

Because Cancer experiences deep emotions, spiritual or mystical practices can help them release what they no longer need. Some might do a simple ritual of writing a worry on a piece of paper and then safely burning or tearing it up, imagining the stress leaving their heart.

Others find solace in water-based rituals, given Cancer's water element. Standing under a gentle shower and picturing emotional heaviness washing away can bring renewal. Some even collect rainwater in a bowl and use it to lightly cleanse items that hold emotional significance. The point is to link symbolic action with the desire to let go of burdens.

Such rituals do not require firm religious belief. They can be personal, meaningful acts that help the mind transition from one emotional state to another. By externalizing the process, Cancer might find it easier to move past stuck feelings.

Spiritual Symbols and Objects

Cancers may feel drawn to objects that carry personal meaning. These might include shells, stones, crystals, or small figurines. Some sense that certain crystals or stones hold energies that can calm the mind or protect from negativity.

Popular stones for Cancer might be moonstone (linked to lunar energy and intuition), rose quartz (often associated with gentle love), or selenite (sometimes seen as purifying). Whether or not one believes in the literal power of stones, holding or looking at them can act as a reminder of emotional aims—like self-love or clarity.

A Cancer might keep these items on a bedside table or in a small pouch to carry around. They might also decorate a special shelf with items gathered from meaningful places—like beach shells, smooth river rocks, or carved tokens. Each piece becomes a symbol of memories, hopes, or comforting energy.

Meditation and Mindful Approaches

Many spiritual paths include meditation or mindfulness, which can resonate with Cancer's reflective side. Meditation might involve sitting quietly and focusing on the breath, repeating a simple phrase, or visualizing a peaceful scene. Over time, it can help calm restless thoughts and strengthen intuition.

Mindfulness is about paying close attention to the present moment. For example, while washing dishes, a Cancer could notice the warmth of the water, the slippery feel of soap, and the sound of water running. By being fully present, they break free from worries about the past or future. Some see this presence as a spiritual practice, uniting daily life with a deeper awareness.

Longer meditations can be done sitting on a cushion, but mini-meditations might last just a minute or two. When emotions run high, stepping aside to close the eyes and take a few calm breaths can shift the internal atmosphere.

Sacred Spaces in the Home

Cancers often thrive when they have a cozy sanctuary. Some might create a small corner or shelf at home that feels sacred in a personal way. This could hold objects like a favorite candle, a meaningful photo, a small plant, or symbolic items tied to their beliefs.

They might call it an altar, a reflection nook, or simply a calm corner. The name does not matter as much as the feeling of respect and stillness it brings. Stepping into that space for a few minutes each day can ground them, offering a sense of stability and spiritual comfort.

Some people also incorporate seasonal changes into their sacred space. For instance, placing fresh flowers in spring or adding small gourds in autumn. By doing so, they stay in tune with nature's cycles, which can mirror internal emotional cycles.

Dreams as Windows into the Unconscious

Because Cancer can be quite imaginative, dreams might carry special weight. Some Cancers recall vivid dream details and sense messages within them—symbols, places, or repeated themes that hint at hidden feelings.

Keeping a dream journal by the bed can help capture these memories before they vanish upon waking. Later, reading through them might reveal patterns—like recurring symbols or emotional tones. A dream about water, for instance, might point to deeper emotional waves. A dream about a locked door might signal unresolved concerns.

Interpreting dreams does not require complicated systems. Sometimes, simply writing them down and reflecting softly on what the dream setting or storyline might represent can offer insight. It is another way for Cancer to explore the layers of their inner world, which can feel mystical or spiritual.

Spiritual Gatherings and Communities

Some Cancers find comfort in joining gatherings that support spiritual reflection. This might include local groups that meet for meditation, yoga, or gentle chanting. If in a religious community, they could take part in shared prayer or community traditions.

The atmosphere of these gatherings matters. Cancers usually prefer warm, welcoming vibes over strict or judgmental settings. They might explore different groups until they find one that aligns with their gentle approach. The benefit is meeting others who also value deeper connections, forming supportive friendships.

Online communities can be an option too, especially if local resources are limited. Virtual meetups or forums dedicated to mindfulness, mystical studies, or spiritual growth can offer lessons and shared experiences. Cancer might find like-minded souls across the globe who understand their emotional depth.

Honoring Ancestry and Family Customs

Many Cancers feel a strong link to family history or cultural roots. They might find spiritual meaning in honoring ancestors, learning about old traditions, or practicing customs passed down through generations. This can be as simple as cooking a traditional dish with care, lighting a candle on special days, or keeping old family photographs in a respectful place.

Some see these actions as a way to keep family energy alive, blending the past with the present. Others might adapt old customs to modern life, finding personal significance in them. This sense of belonging can be deeply comforting, grounding Cancer in a lineage that stretches beyond themselves.

Elements and Nature in Spiritual View

While Cancer is tied to water, the other elements—earth, air, and fire—might also hold meaning. A Cancer might feel close to earth when they garden, to air when they step out on a windy day, or to fire when lighting a small candle for focus. Recognizing the presence of these elements in daily routines can become a quiet spiritual practice.

For instance, if they plant seeds in the ground, they might pause to reflect on how the earth nurtures growth. If they watch a flame flicker, they might think about how fire can transform darkness into light. Each element can serve as a reminder of the natural rhythms that shape life.

Such observations do not require complex rituals. They are simple moments of reflection that can deepen a Cancer's bond with the world around them. In that bond, they may sense a spiritual unity—a feeling that life is woven together in countless visible and invisible ways.

Gentle Divination Methods

Beyond tarot or oracle cards, some Cancers explore other gentle divination tools. Runes, I Ching sticks, or pendulums are examples. They are not about predicting a fixed future but about stirring thought and revealing hidden feelings.

A Cancer might say, "I am uncertain about a decision," then draw a rune or toss I Ching coins. The resulting symbol or text might spark ideas they had not considered. It is a way to consult the inner self through an external prompt.

Because Cancer can be quite intuitive, these methods may resonate if approached with an open, reflective mindset. If nothing else, they encourage pausing, thinking, and engaging the imagination, which can soothe an anxious heart.

Seasonal and Lunar Festivities

Throughout the year, different cultures observe events linked to seasons or the Moon. They could mark each solstice, equinox, or notable lunar date with a quiet reflection, a small candle lighting, or a short walk outdoors.

These moments help them align with nature's cycles. For example, during a winter solstice, a Cancer might focus on inner warmth and hopes for brighter days ahead. During a summer phase, they might appreciate the long daylight that brings vitality. Such observances need not be large gatherings—just mindful acknowledgments of nature's shift.

Writing Affirmations or Prayers

Some Cancers find comfort in writing short affirmations, prayers, or personal statements that link them to spiritual ideals. These can be notes like:

- "I trust my inner wisdom and open my heart to kindness."

- "I release old hurts and embrace new hope."

Placing these statements on a mirror or in a private journal can reinforce positive beliefs. They may choose to read one daily or whisper it before bed, treating it like a gentle vow that shapes their mindset.

For those with a religious background, traditional prayers can be modified to have personal meaning. The aim is to create words that resonate deeply and encourage calm, faith, or emotional healing.

Quiet Service as Spiritual Practice

Service to others can feel deeply spiritual for a Cancer. Helping a neighbor, comforting a lonely friend, or volunteering in a community effort often feels like living out core values of empathy and compassion. Some see this as a sacred act, a way to express kindness in the real world.

The spiritual aspect here is not about public recognition but about acting from a heartfelt place. A Cancer might drop off homemade soup for someone who is ill, or help an older relative with household chores, finding a sense of connection in the process. Each act becomes a bond that links them to humanity.

However, it is important not to overextend or ignore personal limits. Spiritual service should energize, not exhaust. Keeping a balanced approach allows Cancer to continue giving without harming their own well-being.

Connecting with Ancestors Through Stories

Some Cancers feel a pull to learn about relatives who have passed away or older generations they never met. Reading diaries, letters, or hearing stories from older family members can provide a sense of spiritual continuity. It is like realizing one's life is a chapter in a much bigger book.

They might gather family tales and preserve them in a scrapbook. Or they might retell them at family gatherings so that younger ones know where they come from. This practice can be deeply moving, giving a sense that bonds exist beyond physical presence.

If no family is close, adopting symbolic ancestors—historical figures or cultural heroes who represent ideals—can serve a similar purpose. A Cancer might draw inspiration from a poet or humanitarian whose life story resonates with their emotional worldview.

The Pull of Mystical Literature and Media

Books, podcasts, or documentaries on mystical topics—like near-death experiences, energy healing, or historical legends—may fascinate a Cancer. While they might not accept every claim as fact, exploring these areas can fuel a sense of wonder about life's hidden dimensions.

They might read about ancient civilizations or watch shows exploring lost mysteries. The emotional side of Cancer can be stirred by these tales, sensing that every culture has sought answers beyond daily routines. This broadens their perspective and can spark creativity in other areas of life.

Of course, balancing skepticism with openness is wise. Not everything labeled "mystical" is helpful or authentic. Cancer can trust their intuition to sense what genuinely inspires them versus what feels off or manipulative.

Feeling Guided by Signs and Symbols

A butterfly landing on a window or a specific number appearing repeatedly—some Cancers interpret these as signs or messages. They might say, "I keep seeing feathers everywhere. Maybe it is a reminder to stay lighthearted."

This is not about expecting magical solutions but about forming a dialogue with life's small coincidences. It can be reassuring to believe that life whispers hints through everyday moments. Whether it is truly cosmic or just a personal reminder, it often helps Cancer remain mindful and hopeful.

The key is not to obsess over every small event but to stay relaxed. If something feels meaningful, they can note it. If not, they move on. It is a gentle interplay that can add depth to daily experiences.

Balancing Skepticism and Faith

Even a Cancer drawn to spiritual or mystical areas might have doubts. It is natural to wonder if rituals or beliefs hold any real power. This inner debate is part of many people's spiritual path—balancing reason with feelings of wonder.

A healthy approach is to remain open while also applying critical thinking. If a practice helps them find calm or meaning, it may be valid for them personally, even if not proven by science. If a claim feels harmful or exploitative, they can step away.

Cancers can keep a flexible mindset. Their beliefs may shift over time as they learn more about themselves and the world. What matters is that the spiritual aspect they follow or create nurtures their emotional side and aligns with their values.

Using Music or Chanting

Sound can be a powerful form of spiritual expression. Some Cancers might experiment with soft chanting, humming, or singing bowls. These sounds can create vibrations that some believe promote relaxation or healing.

Listening to tranquil music—flutes, chimes, or ambient nature sounds—can also set a reflective mood. It can be used during meditation or as background while journaling. Music can open the heart, stir memories, or soothe stress, making it a helpful tool for Cancer's emotional nature.

Small chanting practices do not require a grand ceremony. A Cancer could choose a short, calming phrase or syllable, repeating it quietly for a minute or two until they feel a sense of balance return.

Contemplating Life's Cycles

A recurring theme in many spiritual paths is the concept of cycles—birth, growth, release, renewal. Cancer might find these cycles mirrored in emotional waves. At times, they feel full of energy, like a bright bloom. At others, they feel a need to retreat and shed old habits, like leaves falling in autumn.

Accepting this cyclical nature can provide peace. They can realize it is normal to have times of expansion and times of rest. Rather than forcing themselves to be cheerful year-round, they can honor phases of introspection. This acceptance can lighten any guilt about having lower-energy seasons, understanding it as part of life's flow.

Guidance Through Symbolic Stories

Fairy tales, myths, and parables from various cultures might speak to Cancer's heart. These stories often hold deeper truths about courage, compassion, or transformation. Reading a myth about a hero who must go through trials can echo personal challenges, reminding Cancer that hard times can lead to insight.

They do not have to view these tales as literal. Instead, they can see them as symbolic maps of emotional or spiritual growth. Reflecting on a story's lesson can be more powerful than reading stiff advice. It taps into imagination, making the lesson resonate in a gentle, memorable way.

Exploring Past-Life or Soul Ideas

Some Cancers are intrigued by ideas like reincarnation or soul connections. They might read books on past-life regression or wonder if certain people in their life have shared a connection before. This does not mean they must fully believe in these concepts, but they might find them intriguing as a framework for understanding deep bonds or unexplained affinities.

Even if these ideas remain speculative, reflecting on them can open the mind to a broader sense of identity. Cancer might say, "Maybe I have an old soul," explaining why they feel strong empathy or intense nostalgia. True or not, it can bring comfort and a sense of belonging to a bigger story.

Staying Grounded in Modern Life

While exploring mystical areas, it is easy to get lost in daydreams. A Cancer who leans strongly into spiritual ideas might forget practical responsibilities or lose track of daily routines. Striking a balance is essential.

Grounding practices include working with the hands—cleaning, cooking, gardening—or keeping track of daily tasks in a planner. These anchor Cancer to the present. They can enjoy the mystery of life without ignoring the real needs of the body, home, or relationships.

Sharing Beliefs with Loved Ones

Sometimes, a Cancer might feel shy about spiritual or mystical interests, fearing that friends or family will judge them. Yet sharing these interests carefully can deepen connections. If the other person is open-minded, they might appreciate learning about the lunar reflections or the meaningful items Cancer keeps at home.

However, not everyone is receptive. Cancer can sense who might be understanding and who might be dismissive. It is fine to keep certain practices personal if sharing them leads to conflict. A small circle of supportive friends can be enough to feel validated.

Artistic Expressions of the Spiritual

Cancers can blend creativity with their spiritual side by making art that reflects mystical ideas. They might paint abstract images of the Moon or draw mandalas representing harmony. Some compose music or poems inspired by visions during quiet times.

Sharing such art can let others see a glimpse of that inner sense of wonder. It can also be a form of personal reflection, turning intangible feelings into forms that can be seen or heard. This creative process itself can feel like a spiritual journey, shaping and clarifying emotional energies.

Using Affirmations with Moon Cycles

Because the Moon is so central for many Cancers, they can use each phase to set or renew personal affirmations. At the new moon, they might pick one goal or wish. Over the following weeks, they keep reminding themselves of that goal, gently taking steps toward it.

When the moon is full, they might reflect on what has been achieved or learned, and decide if anything needs to be released—like self-doubt or a habit that no longer helps. Then, as the moon wanes, they can focus on letting go of clutter or emotional baggage. This cycle-based approach ties practical actions to a natural rhythm.

Respecting Varied Beliefs

Cancers sometimes act as peacemakers when people have different spiritual viewpoints. They can listen empathetically, acknowledging each person's perspective. This skill can foster harmony in families or circles of friends where beliefs diverge.

In their own spiritual search, a Cancer might blend elements from different traditions—taking a bit of meditation from one, a cleansing ritual from another, and family customs from a third. This personalized tapestry can be unique and flexible, changing as they learn.

Experiencing Quiet Magic in Small Moments

Spiritual or mystical insights do not always arrive in grand events. They can show up in quiet moments—like noticing a cloud shaped like a heart, or having a calm feeling while watching the stars. For many Cancers, these subtle glimpses are enough to remind them that life holds wonder.

They might whisper a silent thanks for these small wonders. Over time, such mindfulness can turn everyday activities into sacred experiences. Waking up, seeing sunlight through the window, and feeling grateful for another day can be a tiny but meaningful practice.

CHAPTER 15: BONDS WITH OTHER ZODIAC SIGNS

Astrology often highlights how different zodiac signs relate to one another. For Cancer, known for strong feelings and a nurturing spirit, the bonds with each sign can vary in intriguing ways. In this chapter, we will look at how Cancer might connect with every zodiac sign, from Aries to Pisces, touching on the positives, the challenges, and suggestions for healthy interactions. While people are more than their Sun sign, these broad observations can still offer helpful insights.

It is important to note that real relationships depend on many factors, including personal backgrounds, values, and communication styles. Still, thinking about zodiac pairings can be a fun and sometimes enlightening way to see patterns in how different personalities might mix or clash.

Cancer and Aries (Fire Sign)

Shared Energy vs. Conflicting Ways

Positives: Aries has excitement and boldness, which can pull Cancer out of a shell and bring fresh experiences. Cancer's gentle nature can soften Aries's impulsive streak, showing Aries the value of patience and emotional care.

Challenges: Aries is direct, sometimes blunt, and might not understand Cancer's sensitivity. Meanwhile, Cancer can see Aries's fast decisions as too risky. If Aries speaks harshly or rushes forward without thinking, Cancer might feel hurt.

Tips for Harmony:

- Aries can practice gentle language, remembering Cancer's tender feelings.
- Cancer can be open about feelings without expecting Aries to read unspoken cues.
- Shared activities that blend excitement with comfort can create balance (e.g., a short adventurous outing followed by a quiet dinner at home).

Cancer and Taurus (Earth Sign)

Shared Need for Stability and Warmth

Positives: Both Cancer and Taurus value comfort and consistency. They might enjoy cozy nights cooking meals or taking walks in nature, delighting in shared routines. Cancer appreciates Taurus's steady presence, and Taurus often admires Cancer's homey vibe.

Challenges: Taurus is practical and can be stubborn. Cancer, driven by feelings, might want Taurus to sense emotional shifts without being told. If Taurus is too set in routines, Cancer might feel overlooked when moods change.

Tips for Harmony:

- Talk openly about emotional needs. Taurus can ask, "How can I help?" instead of guessing.
- Keep a peaceful environment with touches of affection. Both signs thrive on calm and physical comfort.

- Plan activities that appeal to senses (e.g., picking fresh fruit, gardening, or enjoying slow afternoons).

Cancer and Gemini (Air Sign)

Meeting of Feeling and Thought

Positives: Gemini brings witty conversation and variety, while Cancer adds depth and empathy. Cancer might enjoy Gemini's stories and playful ideas. In turn, Gemini can learn to listen more closely, developing emotional insight from Cancer.

Challenges: Gemini's restless mind may feel stifled by Cancer's need for familiarity and emotional reassurance. Cancer might see Gemini's shifting interests as a lack of commitment. Misunderstandings can arise if Gemini seems too detached and Cancer gets clingy.

Tips for Harmony:

- Give each other space to handle problems differently: Gemini through logic and Cancer through feelings.
- Engage in group activities that blend fun with emotional closeness, like a game night that ends in heart-to-heart chat.
- Keep communication lively but also respectful of deeper feelings.

Cancer and Cancer (Water Sign)

Reflecting Each Other's Moods

Positives: Two Cancers can create a warm, caring environment, understanding each other's emotional waves without much explanation. They might share strong family values, a love of home life, and a knack for picking up on subtle signals.

Challenges: With so many deep feelings, both might spiral into worry or sadness if one is upset. They could feed each other's anxieties if they do not keep perspective. They also risk staying in a comfort zone too long, avoiding necessary growth.

Tips for Harmony:

- Practice gentle honesty, so both can handle small problems before they become big.
- Make sure to take breaks when emotions run high. A short walk or solitary hobby might keep them from melting into each other's worries.
- Encourage each other to explore new experiences. Growth can happen if they gently push each other beyond a shared shell.

Cancer and Leo (Fire Sign)

Warm Generosity vs. Emotional Sensitivity

Positives: Leo's flair and confidence can brighten Cancer's day, while Cancer's support helps Leo feel adored. Cancer admires Leo's bold warmth, and Leo appreciates Cancer's loyalty. They can form a protective team where both care deeply for each other.

Challenges: Leo likes attention and might unintentionally overlook Cancer's quieter needs. If Leo acts too grand or seeks too much spotlight, Cancer could feel overshadowed. Conflicts can arise if Cancer's moodiness clashes with Leo's pride.

Tips for Harmony:

- Leo can show genuine concern for Cancer's emotions, offering praise and gentle reassurance.

- Cancer can voice needs early, rather than withdrawing and hoping Leo guesses.

- Shared creative pursuits (like planning a small gathering) can satisfy Leo's flair and Cancer's nurturing style.

Cancer and Virgo (Earth Sign)

Practical Care and Emotional Support

Positives: Virgo is detail-focused and can help bring order to Cancer's life, while Cancer provides warmth and a safe space for Virgo's worries. Both value a calm routine and often share a desire to help others.

Challenges: Virgo's critical eye can bruise Cancer's feelings if not phrased softly. Cancer's shifting moods can puzzle Virgo, who might try to fix problems with logic when emotional understanding is needed.

Tips for Harmony:

- Practice patient communication. Virgo can frame suggestions kindly, and Cancer can clarify that they need empathy before solutions.
- Find common ground in tasks like cooking, organizing, or volunteering, which matches both signs' helpful natures.
- Keep a gentle atmosphere where small acts of care are appreciated.

Cancer and Libra (Air Sign)

Finding Balance Between Emotions and Harmony

Positives: Libra is charming and seeks peace, matching well with Cancer's desire for a harmonious home. Cancer enjoys Libra's friendly nature, while Libra admires Cancer's thoughtfulness. They can excel at hosting social get-togethers, blending Libra's grace with Cancer's warm hospitality.

Challenges: Libra sometimes avoids direct conflict, which can frustrate Cancer if serious feelings are not addressed. Cancer's emotional swings might unsettle Libra, who wants a smooth environment. Tension may rise if Libra tries too hard to keep things light and Cancer wants deeper talks.

Tips for Harmony:

- Libra can encourage open emotional discussions instead of glossing over them for politeness.
- Cancer might accept that Libra needs some space for social activities.
- Shared interests in art or music can bond them, as both appreciate gentle beauty.

Cancer and Scorpio (Water Sign)

Intense Connection Through Shared Depth

Positives: Both are water signs, so they can connect on a deep emotional level. Scorpio's passionate approach may draw Cancer out of shyness, and Cancer's nurturing side can soften Scorpio's intensity. Loyalty runs high, creating a sense of strong protection for each other.

Challenges: Scorpio's secretive streak might stir Cancer's insecurities. If Scorpio becomes possessive or Cancer becomes overly clingy, conflicts can heat up quickly. Emotional power struggles might surface if trust is lacking.

Tips for Harmony:

- Build trust by sharing feelings regularly, not letting secrets or resentments pile up.
- Respect each other's need for occasional solitude. Both can hold strong emotions, so quiet breaks prevent overload.
- Channel shared depth into creative projects or private traditions that strengthen their bond.

Cancer and Sagittarius (Fire Sign)

Emotional Roots vs. Exploratory Spirit

Positives: Sagittarius's optimism can uplift Cancer, and Cancer's warmth can provide a home base for Sagittarius to return to. Sagittarius might stir Cancer's curiosity about bigger ideas, while Cancer offers genuine care that helps Sagittarius feel appreciated.

Challenges: Sagittarius loves freedom and might struggle with Cancer's desire for closeness. If Sagittarius roams too freely (physically or mentally), Cancer may feel neglected. Meanwhile, Sagittarius might see Cancer as too clingy or cautious.

Tips for Harmony:

- Balance time apart with meaningful togetherness. Let Sagittarius explore, but keep in touch so Cancer knows they remain important.
- Talk openly about boundaries: how much closeness Cancer craves and how much independence Sagittarius needs.
- Find shared learning activities—maybe a short class or reading group—where they can combine Sagittarius's excitement with Cancer's supportive nature.

Cancer and Capricorn (Earth Sign)

Opposite Signs That Can Form a Solid Axis

Positives: Cancer and Capricorn sit opposite each other in the zodiac, often complementing each other's strengths. Capricorn's discipline and ambition can give Cancer security, while Cancer's empathy reminds Capricorn to slow down and care for emotional needs.

Challenges: Capricorn might focus on goals and come across as too stern, failing to see Cancer's delicate mood shifts. Cancer can become defensive or moody if Capricorn seems unfeeling. Disagreements can stem from Capricorn's practicality vs. Cancer's emotional viewpoints.

Tips for Harmony:

- Acknowledge that each style has value—Capricorn's logic and Cancer's empathy can create a balanced outlook.
- Capricorn can schedule downtime to show they value home life and emotional bonding.

- Work together on building a stable environment. For example, saving money for a comfortable home or planning big goals while respecting each other's feelings.

Cancer and Aquarius (Air Sign)

Emotional Depth vs. Independent Thought

Positives: Aquarius's broad-minded ideas can fascinate Cancer, opening them to social issues or unique perspectives. Cancer's caring nature can soften Aquarius's sometimes distant approach. Both can share a desire to help people, though in different ways.

Challenges: Aquarius values freedom and might seem detached, confusing Cancer, who yearns for deeper emotional connection. Cancer's desire for closeness can clash with Aquarius's wish to remain independent.

Tips for Harmony:

- Establish mutual respect for different approaches: emotional closeness for Cancer, mental space for Aquarius.
- Plan activities that merge each sign's style, like a community service project (helping Cancer feel caring) with an innovative spin (satisfying Aquarius's creativity).
- Clear communication about feelings and personal space can prevent misunderstandings.

Cancer and Pisces (Water Sign)

A Flowing Union of Two Water Signs

Positives: Both signs understand emotional depth. They often connect intuitively, sensing each other's moods. Pisces's dreamy nature and Cancer's caring instincts can create a bond filled with compassion and shared imagination.

Challenges: Both can become overwhelmed by emotions if they lack healthy boundaries. Pisces might seem too lost in fantasies, leaving Cancer to handle practical matters. If sadness hits both at once, it can be hard to stay grounded.

Tips for Harmony:

- Gently support each other's emotions, but keep some structure in daily life so responsibilities do not slip.
- Encourage creative expression or spiritual reflection together.
- Remember to step back if either sign feels drained, so each can recharge before diving into deeper feelings again.

How to Use Zodiac Insights in Real Life

Reading about zodiac sign matches is fun, but it is not a rulebook. People are unique, shaped by upbringing, experiences, and many other astrological factors besides Sun signs (like Moon or rising signs). Still, these general observations can give a starting point for understanding where conflicts might arise or how best to show care.

- **Communicate Clearly**: Regardless of sign, letting people know feelings and needs is vital.

- **Respect Differences**: Each sign has strengths and weaknesses. Recognizing these can prevent harsh judgments.

- **Find Shared Ground**: Look for activities or values that both people enjoy, building a base of goodwill.

Family Bonds Across Signs

In families, a Cancer might have a sibling who is loud (like Aries) or a parent who is quiet (like Virgo). Understanding zodiac patterns can ease frustrations. For instance, if a Cancer teen sees that their Aries sibling simply loves spontaneity, they might not take it personally when that sibling forgets to invite them until the last minute.

Similarly, if a Capricorn parent seems too strict, a Cancer can realize that the parent might be showing love through structure and planning. By noticing these differences, families can learn to appreciate varied strengths. Cancer, with their empathy, might even help relatives see each other more kindly.

Friendships with Different Signs

Friendships often let Cancer explore different perspectives. While water sign friends (Scorpio, Pisces) might readily bond over emotional chats, air sign friends (Gemini, Libra, Aquarius) can bring fresh conversations or group outings. Fire sign companions (Aries, Leo, Sagittarius) may add excitement, pushing Cancer out of comfort zones. Earth signs (Taurus, Virgo, Capricorn) help with stability and practical support.

When forming or keeping friendships:

- **Balance**: If a friend is high-energy, Cancer can request calm hangouts sometimes. If a friend is very logical, Cancer can offer empathy when deeper issues arise.

- **Avoid Stereotypes**: Each friend is still an individual. Using zodiac insights should guide, not box people in.

- **Celebrate Differences**: A friend who is very different can help Cancer grow and see life from new angles.

Romantic Relationships and Compatibility

While romantic compatibility does not only rest on zodiac pairings, these guidelines offer a lighthearted view of which traits might fit naturally and which might need extra effort. For instance:

- **Fire signs** bring spark and can teach Cancer to be bolder, though adjusting to Cancer's emotional pace is key.

- **Earth signs** offer security and practical planning, which Cancer finds comforting, but must mind emotional nuance.

- **Air signs** bring mental stimulation, though they may need to slow down and validate Cancer's feelings.

- **Water signs** feel deeply and understand each other's emotional flow, but risk getting stuck if both are too sensitive at once.

Communication remains the heart of any relationship. If Cancer can express their worries or joys clearly, and the other person can respond with respect, many potential conflicts can be managed.

Working Relationships by Sign

In a work setting, Cancer might find themselves as the caring coworker or manager who notices how everyone feels. How they mesh with each sign can shape team dynamics:

- **With Aries, Leo, Sagittarius**: Suggest fun but structured ways to brainstorm, so emotional needs are not overlooked.

- **With Taurus, Virgo, Capricorn**: Use each other's dependability; Cancer can add empathy to break up tense work patterns.

- **With Gemini, Libra, Aquarius**: Employ creative thinking, but ensure emotional points are not ignored.

- **With Scorpio, Pisces**: Collaborate on deeper tasks requiring empathy, though watch for shared emotional overload.

Tips for Overcoming Sign Clashes

No matter the sign, there can be periods of clash. Some general pointers for Cancer dealing with friction:

1. **Set Boundaries**: If a coworker or friend's style feels overwhelming, politely communicate your limits.

2. **Open Heart, Calm Mind**: Approach conflicts with empathy but stay logical enough to avoid being drained.

3. **Avoid Silent Treatment**: Cancer might retreat when hurt, but explaining feelings early can prevent bigger problems.

4. **Learn Each Other's Language**: Some signs prefer direct talk, others prefer gentle hints. Find a balanced way to share concerns.

Growing from Each Sign Encounter

Every zodiac sign has unique qualities. Cancer can see each interaction as a chance to learn something about themselves or about life:

- **From Fire signs**: Gaining courage and spontaneity.

- **From Earth signs**: Finding stability and patience.

- **From Air signs**: Expanding ideas and communication skills.

- **From Water signs**: Deepening emotional wisdom and mutual support.

This variety can enrich Cancer's worldview, helping them develop a wide range of social and emotional tools. Instead of seeing differences as problems, they can see them as learning opportunities.

Handling Surprises in Sign Pairings

Sometimes, supposedly "perfect" sign matches fail, or "unlikely" pairs thrive. Factors like personal maturity, life goals, and communication habits matter more than simple zodiac labels. Two people might share the same sign but have very different personalities due to rising signs, family upbringing, or other influences.

Cancer, with a flexible and caring spirit, can adapt to various personalities if both parties communicate respectfully. While it helps to keep zodiac tendencies in mind, it should not overshadow direct observation of how someone acts.

Combining Intuition with Sign Insights

Cancer's intuition can play a big role in spotting whether a connection feels right. They might sense that a normally "clashing" sign is surprisingly supportive or that a theoretically "good" match is draining them. By blending these feelings with basic zodiac insights, they can navigate relationships with a balanced approach.

If a friend or partner truly respects and values Cancer's emotional perspective, many sign differences become manageable. Conversely, if Cancer feels disregarded, even a so-called compatible sign might lead to friction. The ultimate guide is the level of empathy and open communication on both sides.

Group Dynamics with Mixed Signs

In a group of varied signs, Cancer might act as the emotional center, noticing who feels left out or stressed. They can do well as a mediator, especially if they learn enough about each sign's style to understand potential triggers. For instance, they might approach a fiery Aries differently than a thoughtful Capricorn.

This ability to sense the group's mood can make Cancer a valued teammate or leader. They can plan gatherings that consider different temperaments—maybe quieter segments for the introverted signs and fun, active parts for the outgoing ones. By blending these, Cancer fosters a balanced atmosphere.

Seeking Support from Specific Signs

When Cancer needs help, they might turn to different signs for different types of support:

- **Emotional empathy**: Water signs (Scorpio, Pisces, another Cancer).

- **Practical advice**: Earth signs (Taurus, Virgo, Capricorn).

- **Excitement or motivation**: Fire signs (Aries, Leo, Sagittarius).

- **Mental clarity**: Air signs (Gemini, Libra, Aquarius).

Knowing which friend or colleague best matches the needed support can simplify turning to the right person at the right time. This is not about limiting who to talk to, but about recognizing each sign's natural gifts.

Handling Criticism from Different Signs

Criticism can sting a sensitive Cancer, so understanding each sign's style might help.

- **Fire signs** may be blunt but well-meaning.

- **Earth signs** might be methodical, focusing on facts.

- **Air signs** could sound detached or too rational.

- **Water signs** may try to be gentle but could still trigger deep emotions.

Cancer can remind themselves that feedback is not a personal attack. They can process it calmly, maybe taking a moment alone to reflect. Explaining how they feel when receiving harsh words is also beneficial, so others can soften their approach next time.

Teaching Others About Sensitivity

Cancer often becomes an example of caring communication. By calmly stating, "I appreciate honest feedback, but I also need kind wording," they show that emotional sensitivity is not weakness—it is just a different style. Some signs might never have thought about how words affect feelings. Cancer's gentle reminders can raise everyone's emotional awareness.

This teaching can happen at work, at home, or among friends. Over time, people might adopt better listening skills, leaving less room for misunderstandings. Cancer's role as an empathetic guide can improve group harmony.

Finding Joy in Unlikely Pairings

Sometimes, the greatest friendships or romances happen between signs that are not commonly viewed as "easy matches." Perhaps a lively Sagittarius helps Cancer discover a new zest for life, or an Aquarius broadens Cancer's social circle.

By staying open, Cancer can find unexpected joys. The trick is acknowledging differences early on. If they see, for example, that a partner is highly independent, they can talk about how to maintain closeness without smothering. This approach fosters respect on both sides.

Learning Self-Reliance and Growth

No matter the sign connections, Cancer might learn over time that relationships flourish when each person also does personal self-care. If Cancer leans too heavily on a partner or friend for emotional security, it can strain the bond.

Balancing close ties with a sense of self-reliance often enhances relationships rather than weakening them. Each sign might have something to teach Cancer about standing on their own feet. For example, Aries's courage can inspire Cancer to face fears. Virgo's organization can motivate Cancer to plan daily tasks. Each sign can be a teacher.

Keeping Realistic Expectations

Expecting a certain sign to act one way all the time is risky. People evolve. A once-shy Taurus could become more adventurous. A boisterous Leo could mellow out. Cancer thrives best when staying flexible, responding to who the person is now rather than clinging to rigid zodiac rules.

It helps to observe real changes in a relationship. If a Libra friend used to be hesitant to talk about tough feelings but is now more open, Cancer can adapt and encourage that growth. This dynamic approach ensures that bonds remain alive rather than stuck in old patterns.

CHAPTER 16: CULTURAL STORIES AND LEGENDS

Many ancient cultures gazed at the sky and noted the movements of celestial bodies. Over time, they created stories, myths, and legends to explain these patterns. The constellation of Cancer—represented by the crab—found its place in various tales around the world. Though the details differ, the main idea remains that people have long tried to link star formations to events on Earth or to symbolic characters.

In this chapter, we will explore how different societies have interpreted the Cancer constellation, as well as crab-related myths that might resonate with the sign's traits. We will also look at how these legends shaped traditions, artwork, and thought, showing the deep bond between humans and the stars above.

The Greek Myth of the Crab in Hercules's Labors

A well-known story comes from ancient Greece, where the hero Hercules (also called Heracles) faced a series of challenges. One of his tasks was to defeat the Hydra, a serpent-like beast with many heads. During this battle, a crab is said to have tried to help the Hydra.

The Crab's Role

- The crab pinched Hercules's foot, hoping to distract him.
- Hercules, annoyed by the crab, crushed it underfoot.

- The goddess Hera, who disliked Hercules, was grateful to the crab for its attempt to help the Hydra. She placed the crab in the sky as the constellation Cancer.

Although the crab was not victorious, its loyalty and courage gained a place among the stars. Ancient storytellers said that this myth showed how even small creatures can find immortality through noble efforts.

For people who identify with Cancer, this tale might reflect a willingness to protect those they care about, even when facing great odds. While the crab's fate was grim in the story, the crab's memory lived on in the sky, hinting at themes of devotion and hidden bravery.

Connections to the Moon in Different Cultures

Because Cancer is linked to the Moon in astrology, many stories tie the crab or the Cancer constellation to lunar themes. In some cultures, the Moon was seen as a symbol of change or emotion, much like Cancer itself.

Myths and Lunar Cycles

In certain ancient societies, the Moon was viewed as a goddess figure, overseeing tides, growth, and emotional rhythms.

Some tales said that a crab or similar creature guarded the Moon's secrets, acting as a gatekeeper between land and water.

While the exact details shift from one region to another, the shared idea is that the crab stands near the watery, reflective qualities of the Moon. People who felt drawn to Cancer might see themselves as watchers of tides—both ocean tides and emotional tides in the heart.

Egyptian and Babylonian Perspectives

Early civilizations like the Egyptians and Babylonians also mapped the stars, developing star catalogs that influenced later Greek and Roman astrology.

In ancient Egypt, the constellation sometimes appeared as scarabs (sacred beetles) rather than crabs. The scarab symbolized rebirth and transformation, tying to the idea of the sun's daily renewal. Though not exactly the crab we know, the concept of a shelled creature connected to cyclical change is similar to Cancer's main traits.

In Babylonian astronomy, certain star groups were linked with watery themes. While the exact link to a crab shape is not always clear, the Babylonians recognized constellations that eventually merged into the Greek zodiac system.

These glimpses show that the idea of a crab or a shelled creature in the sky existed in multiple star traditions, sometimes melding with local symbols or sacred animals.

Crab Symbols in Ancient Mythologies

Beyond the constellation, crabs appear in various mythologies worldwide, often symbolizing protection, adaptability, or a connection to the sea.

In some Polynesian tales, crabs were seen as caretakers of shores, cleaning up debris and representing the boundary between land and ocean.

In East Asian folklore, crabs might appear in stories about cunning or resilience, using their claws in unexpected ways to solve problems.

In certain African legends, the crab is portrayed as wise, warning others about dangers hidden in muddy waters.

While these do not always tie directly to the zodiac sign Cancer, they highlight how different cultures have respected the crab's qualities. The crab's shell—hard on the outside, soft within—can symbolize both defense and vulnerability.

The Constellation Cancer Through History

The name "Cancer" comes from the Latin word for crab. Astronomers long ago saw a cluster of stars that seemed to form the shape (though faintly) of a crab in the night sky. This cluster moved through the ecliptic, the path the Sun appears to follow over a year. Hence, it became part of the zodiac belt.

Dim but Significant

Cancer is sometimes known as a dim constellation, not as bright as Leo or Taurus.

Despite its faintness, it carries special importance because it marks a cardinal point in some astrological traditions (the start of northern summer).

Throughout medieval and Renaissance Europe, star charts often depicted a crab or crayfish to represent Cancer. Artists drew elaborate shapes to show the creature in manuscripts or celestial globes. Over time, these images reinforced the idea of Cancer as part of the zodiac "family" recognized across continents.

The Tropic of Cancer

Geographically, the Tropic of Cancer is an imaginary line circling the Earth, at about 23.5 degrees north of the Equator. It got its name because, in ancient times, the Sun was in the constellation Cancer at the June solstice (the start of summer in the northern hemisphere).

Cultural Influence

Regions along the Tropic of Cancer, such as parts of Mexico, Africa, and Asia, have significant historical ties to solar events. Festivals or important rituals might occur around the solstice, linking the sun's peak to the crab sign.

While the Sun's exact position has shifted slightly due to the precession of Earth's axis, the name "Tropic of Cancer" remains a cultural marker. It reminds us of how the zodiac once served as a practical guide to seasonal changes.

In symbolic terms, the Tropic of Cancer stands for a turning point—where the Sun is at its farthest point north. For Cancer folks, it might feel like a metaphor for stepping into a phase of warmth and growth, paralleling emotional blossoming.

Hindu Astrology (Vedic Tradition)

In Hindu or Vedic astrology, the sign corresponding to Cancer is called Karka (or Karkata in some texts). While there are overlaps with Western astrology, differences in calculation exist due to sidereal versus tropical systems.

Karka Sign Themes

Often linked to nurturing, home life, and strong feelings.

Seen as a water sign ruled by the Moon, reflecting similar emotional associations.

In some Vedic stories, creatures like the crab or turtle might appear as forms of deities who maintain cosmic order. Though not always direct parallels to Cancer, these tales show how watery or shelled animals are connected to divine protection.

Chinese and East Asian Constellations

In traditional Chinese astronomy, the sky is divided differently than the Western zodiac. Still, certain star groups in the same region as Cancer have names that suggest smaller animals or objects.

One grouping known as the "Ghost" (in Chinese tradition) overlaps with part of the Cancer constellation.

The concept of the "Four Symbols" in Chinese myth includes the Azure Dragon, Vermilion Bird, White Tiger, and Black Tortoise, each ruling a portion of the sky. While none is a crab, the emphasis on animals as cosmic guardians mirrors the idea of creature constellations in Western lore.

East Asian star lore is rich and varied, with some areas matching Western zodiac paths and others diverging. For a Cancer person exploring these myths, it can be fun to see how the idea of animals in the stars resonates across different lands.

The Beehive Cluster (Praesepe)

Within Cancer lies a notable cluster of stars known as the Beehive Cluster or Praesepe, which means "manger" in Latin. Ancient astrologers saw this small group of stars as a cloudy patch.

Symbolic Interpretations

In old texts, it was called the "Manger" or "Crib," sometimes linked to nurturing or birth.

For those with telescopes, it looks like a swarm of stars, which is why modern astronomy calls it the Beehive.

The presence of the Beehive Cluster in Cancer adds another layer of meaning—some see it as a cosmic cradle, tying back to Cancer's themes of home and caring. While these interpretations are symbolic rather than literal, they resonate with the sign's nurturing image.

Crabs in Folklore: Adaptation and Tenacity

Across many cultures, crabs are admired for adapting to changing tides, moving sideways, and shielding themselves with a tough exterior. Folklore often points to these traits:

Adaptation: Crabs scuttle between land and sea, suggesting versatility.

Tenacity: Once a crab grips something in its claw, it can hold on firmly—mirroring Cancer's loyalty and determination.

Home and Shell: The crab's shell is a mobile home, reminiscent of Cancer's love for secure personal space.

In some local legends, people have used the crab's symbolism to teach lessons about resilience or caution. For example, a story might warn children not to venture too far into the water alone, using a crab character that demonstrates the balance between curiosity and safety.

Stories and Holidays Linked to June and July

Cancer typically covers birthdays from around June 21 to July 22. In parts of the northern hemisphere, this marks the shift into summer. Many regions have seasonal celebrations at this time, though the specific word for these events must be avoided here.

- In older agrarian societies, this was a time of long days, warm weather, and gatherings connected to growth or harvest cycles.

- Some coastal areas might have recognized crab-fishing or shellfish traditions, tying local wildlife to seasonal feasting.

Though not always directly referencing the zodiac, these local customs add to the cultural fabric around the time Cancer is in the Sun's position, reinforcing the sign's link to nourishment, warmth, and familial gatherings (in a broad sense).

Crab Legends in Modern Pop Culture

Modern culture still features crabs in various forms—cartoons, comics, and stories. Characters with crab-like traits might appear shy or defensive, only revealing a caring side under the shell. Some might show fierce loyalty, standing up for friends despite smaller size.

In anime or fantasy stories, a crab-person or crustacean-like guardian might protect a coastal kingdom. This echoes old myths, where crabs guarded or fought alongside greater beings. While these fictional tales often stray from classical myths, they continue the idea that crabs embody both caution and courage.

Sea Myths and the Protective Crab

Seafaring cultures often had myths of crabs or related creatures helping sailors or acting as omens. For instance, seeing a crab near the shore might mean safe fishing conditions or signal that the tides were shifting.

Some boatmakers carved crab symbols on vessels for protection, believing the crab's shell was a sign of shielded fortune at sea. Though these practices vary widely, they reveal a shared respect for crab-like defenders.

Symbolism in Art and Emblems

Over centuries, painters and sculptors have used the crab motif to represent secrecy, self-defense, or emotional depth. In certain emblem books of the Renaissance, a crab might stand for loyalty or caution.

Heraldry, the art of creating coats of arms, also occasionally features crabs. Families with ties to coastal regions or fishing might include a crab as a crest symbol, reflecting local identity or protective values. These artistic choices keep the crab's image alive in visual tradition, reminding viewers of its layered meaning.

Crab Ceremonies in Island Communities

Some island communities hold small-scale ceremonies where crabs play a role—such as releasing them into the sea as a sign of respect for marine life. Though not always tied to the Cancer constellation, these events echo the bond between humans and crustaceans.

In a few places, children learn how to catch crabs gently, observe them, and release them back. This fosters respect for nature and highlights how crabs maintain the shoreline ecosystem by cleaning debris. Such learning experiences pass on the idea that crabs deserve care for the balance they bring.

The Crab's Hard Shell in Storytelling

In literature, a crab's shell is sometimes used as a metaphor for being guarded or shy. Writers draw parallels between a character who hides behind a tough exterior and a crab huddling in its shell. Over time, that character might open up, just as a crab might step out to explore.

For Cancers reading such stories, the metaphor may ring true. The shell can feel like a safe place, but it can also limit seeing the world. Tales where a character learns to trust or connect with others can reflect Cancer's own need for balance between self-protection and emotional sharing.

Cultural Fusion and Modern Festivals

As cultures interact, new forms of celebration emerge, blending local traditions with references to zodiac signs. Some modern events highlight the 12 zodiac constellations, with each sign receiving special mention during its time of year.

Cancer might be given a crab mascot or a watery theme, possibly hosting beach cleanups or seafood tastings that promote coastal care. In these fused celebrations, old legends meet modern environmental or community goals, keeping the spirit of the crab relevant and rooted in caring values.

Comparing Cancer Tales to Other Creatures

Each zodiac sign has an animal or symbol—like Aries's ram, Taurus's bull, or Scorpio's scorpion. Cancer's crab is often contrasted with these other creatures. While some are land-based or fierce, the crab merges land and water, symbolizing the in-between realm where emotions (water) meet daily life (land).

When studied together, the zodiac animals form a wide tapestry of traits—bravery, patience, curiosity, etc. The crab stands out for its protective shell and link to tides, which ties neatly into the broader theme of cyclical change found in ancient stories.

Lessons from Global Crab Legends

From all these stories and cultural angles, certain lessons emerge that speak to Cancer's nature:

Defense and Protection: Crabs show that defense is not necessarily aggression. It can be a careful choice to guard what matters.

Loyalty and Devotion: In the Hercules myth, the crab sided with the Hydra out of loyalty to Hera. This act, though small, was immortalized.

Adaptation: Many cultures see crabs as symbols of flexibility, living in varied environments and shifting with tides.

Emotional Connection: The watery link often associates crabs with feelings, hinting that sensitivity can be powerful rather than weak.

Astronomy and Astrology: A Blended Heritage

Astronomy is the study of celestial objects, while astrology interprets them for human traits. Historically, they were once entwined, with stargazers charting cosmic movements to shape myths and daily practices. Cancer, as a constellation and an astrological sign, stands at that crossing of science and storytelling.

Over centuries, improvements in telescopes and space exploration taught us more about stars, yet the old stories persist. Some see them as poetic or spiritual, others as cultural records of how humans made sense of the universe. For Cancer, these tales offer a heritage that underscores the sign's caring and intuitive identity.

The Crab in Poetry and Music

Poets through the ages sometimes used crab imagery to represent sidelong motion or hidden feelings. A line might refer to "moving sideways like a crab" to describe a hesitant person. Musicians might craft songs about tides and crabs, evoking the slow rhythms of water and emotion.

Contemporary music, especially in coastal regions, might reference crabs as a symbol of local pride. Folkloric chants or sea shanties can mention crabs as part of fishing life. Even if not directly about Cancer astrology, these references keep the crab in public consciousness as a mystical or meaningful creature.

Cultural Ceremonies Honoring Zodiac Animals

In some parts of the world, all 12 zodiac animals (in the Western sense) might receive symbolic tributes during the year. For Cancer's turn, local groups might organize small gatherings discussing the crab's meaning—strength in silence, family devotion, or ties to the Moon.

Speakers could share old myths or personal stories of times they felt "like a crab," needing to guard themselves or step out with caution. Such events preserve the link between old cultural lore and modern identity, showing how myths continue to shape our sense of self.

Reflecting Personal Stories in Crab Legends

Because the crab has that dual nature—tough outside, soft inside—people with strong Cancer traits might find parallels in these global stories. A shy child might see themselves in the little crab that clings to the shore, uncertain but curious about the sea. An adult might recall a time they "pinched" a problem by standing up for a loved one, even if it meant risking their own comfort.

These mythic connections can bring comfort. Realizing that countless generations told crab tales to teach courage, loyalty, or caution can help a modern Cancer see their sensitivities as part of a long tradition. The star-based myths become something personal, not just distant legends.

Legends of Compassion and Sacrifice

In some lesser-known stories, a crab might offer assistance to a lost traveler or wounded animal, giving up its shell or guiding them across treacherous terrain. Though these might be short folktales, the theme is often compassion—helping others despite being small or misunderstood.

Such stories echo Cancer's compassionate side. They remind us that even if we feel powerless, an act of kindness can make a difference.

The crab's shell is not just for personal defense but can also shield others. By linking these legends to daily life, Cancer can find role models for empathy.

Modern Art and Symbolic Tattoos

Today, some people choose crab or Cancer-themed tattoos to honor their star sign or personal traits. Artists might paint or sculpt crabs in styles that blend ancient imagery with modern design. This art often emphasizes the crab's shape—claws, shell, and the subtle curve suggesting sideways motion.

Such expressions keep the old myths alive in fresh ways. A person might wear a crab tattoo as a statement of loyalty or emotional depth, linking themselves to a storied past. Others might collect crab-themed art pieces, feeling a bond with that symbolism.

Cultural Adaptations in Children's Literature

Children's books sometimes feature a friendly crab that learns about bravery or friendship. These tales borrow from older myths but simplify them for young readers. For instance, a crab might be shy about dancing but eventually finds confidence when it sees other creatures supporting it.

These stories foster empathy early on, showing kids that it is okay to move at their own pace (sideways if needed!). By relating to a crab character, young readers can grasp the idea of using caution while still participating in the world—reflecting a key Cancer lesson.

Mythical Journeys of the Crab Hero

In some fantasy settings (games, comics, or novels), a crab hero might embark on quests across watery realms, battling bigger foes or saving an underwater city. While these are modern inventions, they draw on old archetypes: the small but determined crab stepping up to protect a place it loves.

Such narratives highlight courage in unlikely forms. The crab hero's shield might be its shell, representing the concept of home or heart. When adversity strikes, the hero's resilience shines, echoing the Hercules story's idea that even a small being can make an impact.

Universal Themes in Crab Myths

Gathering all these myths and cultural stories, we see certain universal themes:

Balance of Land and Sea: The crab lives in two worlds, suggesting a blend of emotional depths (sea) and daily life (land).

Protection vs. Openness: The shell can keep threats away, but it can also limit connections. Many crab stories revolve around deciding when to hide and when to reach out.

Loyalty and Service: Whether helping Hydra or assisting travelers, crabs often display devotion, even at personal cost.

Symbol of Cycles: Linked to tides, the Moon, and changing phases, the crab teaches that shifts are natural.

For those who resonate with Cancer, these myths form a mirrored reflection of their inner feelings—a confirmation that humans have long seen value in emotional sensitivity and thoughtful defense.

CHAPTER 17: HEALTH TIPS

Cancer is often portrayed as an emotional and caring sign, but these traits can sometimes affect physical and mental health in unique ways. Because of the Cancer sign's sensitivity, stress or worries can build up, leading to potential aches, energy lows, or emotional strain. This chapter focuses on practical health suggestions that can help people who identify with Cancer's qualities—though anyone can benefit from these tips.

We will look at simple approaches to physical well-being, including routine checkups, mindful eating, and balanced exercise. We will also explore how emotions tie into health, pointing out ways to handle stress and maintain a calm mind. These pointers are not medical advice from a doctor but general guidelines that may help a caring, sometimes anxious sign to stay healthy.

The Link Between Emotions and the Body

Cancer is known for deep feelings. Sometimes, holding in strong emotions can lead to stomach aches, tight muscles, or tension headaches. While this can happen to anyone, a Cancer might sense these effects more strongly.

When stress grows, the body produces hormones like cortisol, which can cause fatigue or make it harder to rest. Over time, this state of high alert can weaken the immune system. People who identify with Cancer's traits might notice that if they carry others' problems too much, they start feeling sick or run-down.

Helpful Steps

Daily Emotional Check-Ins: Spend a minute or two each day asking, "How do I feel right now?" Write it down or think about it. If tension is high, take a small step (like a short breathing exercise) to let it out.

Physical Reminders: If the shoulders are hunched or the jaw feels clenched, these might be signs of hidden stress. Try rolling the shoulders or doing a gentle massage to remind the body to relax.

Stress Management for Cancer

Because Cancer can be sensitive to other people's moods, certain environments may increase stress. Crowded workspaces, tense relationships, or constant demands can wear down emotional reserves.

Ways to Manage Stress

Set Boundaries: Politely say "I can't handle this right now" when too many tasks or emotional burdens pile up. Doing so prevents burnout.

Regular Breaks: Plan small breaks through the day—like a brief walk or a quick stretch—to reset the mind.

Relaxation Techniques: Breathing exercises, gentle yoga, or quiet music can lower stress hormones. Even five minutes of mindful calm can make a difference.

Supportive Circles: Seek out friends or groups who understand emotional ups and downs. Sharing concerns can lighten the load.

Routine Checkups and Preventive Care

One key step in staying healthy is attending regular medical, dental, and vision checkups. Cancer sometimes focuses so much on caring for others that they forget their own checkups. Making a schedule for routine visits can help catch small issues before they become big problems.

Ideas for Prevention

Annual or Biannual Checkups: Even if you feel fine, check in with your primary doctor. Ask about blood pressure, weight, and any lingering aches.

Dental Visits: Gum health and clean teeth can impact overall health. Skipping the dentist might lead to costly fixes later.

Eye Care: If you notice headaches when reading or working on screens, an eye exam might reveal the need for updated glasses or simple rest strategies.

Since Cancer can worry a lot, hearing "Everything looks good" from a professional can be a relief. Even if a concern arises, early action usually leads to better outcomes.

Sleep and Rest: A Big Deal for Cancer

Sleep is vital for everyone, but especially for signs that feel daily stresses more sharply. Lack of rest might increase mood swings, lower the immune system, and feed anxiety. On the flip side, good sleep can stabilize emotions and let the body repair itself.

Better Sleep Tips

Regular Bedtime: Going to bed and waking up at the same hours helps regulate the internal clock.

Pre-Bed Ritual: Dim lights, quiet music, or reading a gentle book can signal the mind to slow down.

Screen Limits: Phones or TVs in bed can keep the brain active, leading to poor sleep. Turning off screens at least 30 minutes before bedtime helps.

Comfortable Setup: Invest in pillows or bedding that feel good. For a Cancer who loves a cozy environment, a soft blanket or calming scents might improve rest.

Nutrition and Eating Habits

Because Cancer often enjoys home life, cooking can be both a hobby and a way to stay healthy. Home-cooked meals let you choose fresh ingredients and control added sugars or fats. That said, emotional eating can be a trap if stress leads to craving sweets or heavy meals.

Balanced Eating Advice

Include Many Colors: Different colored fruits and veggies bring varied vitamins.

Watch Emotional Snacking: If stress triggers eating chocolate or chips, look for alternatives—like cut-up veggies with a dip—or try a short walk to relax instead of grabbing food right away.

Stay Hydrated: Water is crucial, especially for a water sign. Aim for a few cups of plain water a day. If plain water is dull, add a slice of lemon or cucumber for taste.

Moderation: Enjoy treats in small amounts rather than banning them, which can cause cravings. If you love sweets, maybe keep them for special times, focusing on mindful enjoyment rather than mindless snacking.

Gentle Exercise for a Water Sign

While some signs thrive on intense sports, Cancer might prefer gentler forms of movement that do not jar the joints or overwhelm the mind. Staying active is key to heart health, mood balance, and weight control.

Possible Activities

Swimming: Water-based exercise can feel natural for a water sign, easing tension on joints while giving a full-body workout.

Yoga or Pilates: These help flexibility and core strength. The slow, mindful aspect can soothe a restless mind.

Walking: A relaxing walk in a park or along a beach can blend exercise with nature's calm.

Dancing: Light dance classes or just moving to music at home can lift spirits without high impact.

The goal is consistency. Even short sessions a few times a week can make a difference in mood and energy. If group workouts feel stressful, solo sessions or small classes might be more comfortable.

Handling Digestive Sensitivities

Some Cancers report having sensitive stomachs, possibly due to stress or emotional tension. Bloating, heartburn, or irregular bowel movements can become worse when anxiety flares.

Stomach-Friendly Habits

Regular Meal Times: Eating at consistent hours helps the digestive system function smoothly.

Light Dinners: Huge, heavy meals at night can disrupt sleep and cause acid reflux.

Gentle Foods: If you feel upset or anxious, mild items like bananas, rice, or soups can be easier to digest.

Avoid Overeating: Large portions can strain the system. Eating slowly and stopping when full can ease stomach tension.

If digestive issues become chronic, speaking to a healthcare provider is wise. They might suggest tests or recommend dietary changes.

Balancing Time Alone and Social Health

Being around others can be nurturing, but too much social activity might overwhelm a Cancer's natural need for quiet recharge. On the other hand, too much alone time can lead to isolation. Striking a balance is important for mental and emotional health, which also affects physical well-being.

Strategies

Plan Social Events Wisely: Space them out rather than cramming everything into a single weekend.

Schedule Quiet Time: Block out hours to read, rest, or do a calm hobby without social demands.

Mindful of Overcommitment: Cancer might say yes to many invites out of kindness. Learn to say no gently if you already feel drained.

Maintaining positive connections can also act as a buffer against stress. A trusted friend's encouraging words might lower tension before it turns physical.

Emotional Release as a Health Measure

Sometimes, tears can be a form of relief. Letting out sadness or frustration in a safe environment (like a private room or with a supportive friend) can prevent bottled-up emotion from causing bigger issues. For Cancer, who might try to shield others from their feelings, learning healthy ways to release tears or vent can be crucial.

Safe Release Options

Writing: Journaling can organize swirling thoughts, turning them into words and clarifying how you feel.

Art: Drawing or painting your mood can serve as a non-verbal release.

Music: Singing or playing an instrument can soothe anxious energy.

Talking: A friend, family member, or counselor can hear you out, providing empathy and guidance.

Managing Anxiety and Worry

Constant worrying can lead to sleep troubles, stomach issues, and a tense posture. Cancer's protective nature might cause concern over loved ones' problems too, adding extra mental strain. Learning ways to handle worry is key to overall health.

Helpful Techniques

Set "Worry Time": Allow 10-15 minutes a day to think about concerns, then focus on other things. This limits how much worry spills into the rest of the day.

Problem-Solving Step by Step: If a worry can be fixed, break it into smaller tasks. If it is out of your control, practice letting go.

Visual Soothers: Some Cancers find mental imagery helpful—picturing waves carrying away fears or imagining a calm beach can steady the mind.

Seek Support: Sharing worries with a sympathetic friend or counselor can lessen the mental load. They might offer another viewpoint or reassurance.

Building a Healthy Relationship with Technology

Excessive screen time can drain energy, disturb sleep, and raise anxiety, especially if reading upsetting news or dealing with social media conflicts. For a sensitive sign, constant online chatter can feel emotionally heavy.

Balanced Tech Use

Screen Curfew: Stop using devices 30–60 minutes before bedtime to help the brain unwind.

Social Media Limits: Set daily time caps. Avoid doom-scrolling through negative content.

Choose Calming Content: Follow accounts that spread positive messages or creative ideas rather than constant drama.

Tech-Free Breaks: Take short breaks during the day to step away from phone alerts.

Creating a Calming Living Space for Health

A messy or harsh environment might raise stress, while a cozy, tidy home can soothe a Cancer's mind. Since the home is often a retreat for this sign, some care in designing the living space can support health.

Home Tips

Gentle Colors: Soft hues on walls or in decoration can relax the eyes.

Minimal Clutter: Keep surfaces clear, storing items in labeled boxes or cabinets.

Touch of Nature: Houseplants or flowers can bring calm vibes, reminding you of growth and freshness.

Aromatherapy: Light scents like lavender or chamomile, but be cautious if you have respiratory sensitivities. Choose well-ventilated spaces for candles or diffusers.

With a calm home, it is easier to unwind after a tough day, supporting emotional stability that ripples into physical well-being.

Mindful Posture and Body Awareness

Slouching or staying hunched over can trap tension in the back and shoulders, leading to chronic soreness. Cancers, especially during emotional states, might shrink in or round the shoulders to guard the chest. Regular posture checks can prevent long-term aches.

Methods to Improve Posture

Shoulder Rolls: Roll shoulders forward and back for a few seconds, then let them relax in a comfortable neutral position.

Neck Stretches: Gently tilt the head to each side, holding the stretch briefly. Avoid jerking or intense pulling.

Back Supports: At work or home, use a supportive chair or a cushion to keep the spine aligned.

Frequent Standing Breaks: If you sit for hours, stand up every 30 minutes to stretch or walk a bit.

Over time, improved posture can make you feel more open, both physically and emotionally.

Health Benefits of a Connection with Nature

Cancer often finds solace near water—lakes, rivers, oceans, or even a backyard pond. The sound of waves or the gentle flow of water can lower stress hormones and clear mental fog. If water access is not available, any natural setting can still be healing.

Tips for Nature Time

Short Walks: Even a 10-minute stroll in a local park can refresh the mind.

Gardening: Growing herbs or flowers can offer a calm activity, connecting you to the earth.

Picnics: Plan a simple snack outdoors. Fresh air helps with relaxation and vitamin D intake from sunlight.

Nature Sounds Indoors: If going outside is difficult, soft recordings of waves or rain can recreate a soothing ambiance.

Balanced Social Lives

Cancer's caring side can mean stepping in whenever someone is in need. While generosity is admirable, too much can lead to exhaustion. If a friend or family member leans on Cancer constantly, Cancer might neglect their own rest.

Guidelines for Healthy Giving

Know Your Limits: Before offering to help, check your own energy level. If already worn out, politely explain that you must recharge first.

Delegate or Suggest Other Avenues: If you cannot help, direct the person to someone else or to a resource that might fix the problem.

Practice "Both/And": You can care about someone's problem while also taking care of yourself. These are not contradictory.

Self-Reward: After helping, treat yourself to something calming—a bath, a quiet read—to restore emotional balance.

Mental Health and the Value of Counseling

Because Cancer can be prone to worry or deep sadness, counseling or therapy might help in tough periods. A counselor can teach coping skills, offer emotional support, and provide an outside view that might clarify confusion.

Signs It Might Help

- Constant low mood or anxiety that lasts for weeks.
- Problems with sleeping or eating patterns.
- Strained relationships because of mood swings or tension.
- Feeling stuck, hopeless, or unable to handle daily tasks.

A mental health professional can guide Cancer through stress, family issues, or self-esteem concerns, improving both emotional and physical well-being.

Finding Purpose in Activity

Engaging in purposeful activities can lift a Cancer's spirit. This might involve volunteering, creative projects, or learning new skills. Feeling a sense of contribution can boost mental health, indirectly aiding physical health.

Ways to Find Purpose

Community Groups: Help at a local shelter, library, or community garden.

Hobby Clubs: Join a small group that shares your interest, like a painting circle or cooking class.

Skill-Building: Sign up for short courses, improving something you have always wanted to learn.

These activities channel emotional energy into constructive tasks, reducing ruminating thoughts that lead to stress.

Tracking Progress and Setting Realistic Goals

For overall health, setting small, doable goals can keep motivation up. Cancer might aim to walk three times a week, try a new recipe, or do a short relaxation session daily. Writing these down or placing them on a calendar can track progress.

Goal-Setting Tips

Start Small: If you have not been exercising, aim for brief walks rather than jumping straight to hour-long routines.

Be Flexible: If a day is too hectic, adjust. One missed walk does not mean failure.

Reward Yourself: Each time you meet a mini-goal, do something nice—like sipping a favorite tea or reading a chapter of a pleasant book.

Celebrate Gains Over Time: Noticing improvements (like better mood or more energy) can keep you going.

Handling Physical Pain or Tension

If physical pain arises—like chronic headaches, backaches, or muscle tension—try not to ignore it. While occasional discomfort might be minor, repeated pains can signal an underlying issue.

Approaches

Home Remedies: Heating pads or light stretches for muscle tension, mild over-the-counter meds if necessary, but check with a professional if pain persists.

Medical Input: If pains last longer than expected, consult a doctor. Early diagnosis can prevent complications.

Stress Link: Sometimes aches are partly stress-related. Relaxation methods or therapy can reduce the frequency or intensity of pain if stress is a major factor.

Listening to the body's signals is part of healthy self-care. A sensitive sign like Cancer might notice pain early, giving an advantage if addressed soon.

Protecting Eyes and Ears

With so much time spent on screens or in noisy environments, eyes and ears can suffer. Eye strain might cause headaches, and loud sounds over time can reduce hearing quality.

Simple Prevention

Screen Breaks: Every 20 minutes, look away from the screen to something far away for about 20 seconds (the "20-20-20 rule").

Adjust Brightness: Reduce screen glare or brightness to a comfortable level.

Volume Control: Keep music or TV at a moderate volume. If in a very loud area, consider earplugs or noise-canceling headphones.

Ear Checkups: If you notice ringing in the ears (tinnitus) or have trouble hearing others, get a hearing test.

Periodic Digital Detox

For a sign that values emotional security, a flood of online updates can destabilize. Scheduling brief digital detox periods—like a weekend offline or at least half a day—can refresh the mind.

Detox Steps

Announce Quiet Time: Let close friends or family know you will be offline so they do not worry.

Plan Offline Fun: Prepare books, art supplies, or a list of errands so you do not default to phone use from boredom.

Journal the Experience: Note how you feel without constant digital pings. Many find they sleep better or think more clearly.

Hydration and Water Healing

Being a water sign, Cancer might already like water, but it is worth emphasizing the health effects of good hydration. Water aids digestion, helps regulate body temperature, and transports nutrients. If feeling sluggish or having headaches, it might be related to insufficient fluids.

Extra Water Touchpoints

Flavored Water: If plain water is dull, add fruit slices (lemon, strawberry, or cucumber).

Warm Baths: Aside from drinking water, a warm bath can soothe aches and calm the mind. Salt baths may help sore muscles.

Foot Soaks: If a full bath is not possible, a quick foot soak can relieve tension, especially at the end of a stressful day.

Sunshine and Vitamin D

Spending time in natural sunlight supports vitamin D production, important for bones and immune function. A short daily exposure (10–15 minutes) can be beneficial, though be mindful of skin protection.

If you live in a region with limited sunlight, a doctor might suggest supplements or recommend more vitamin-D-rich foods (like fatty fish or fortified milk). As always, balance is key: too much direct sun can damage the skin, so moderate exposure is best.

Keeping a Health Journal

Since Cancer can be detail-oriented about feelings, a health journal might expand that approach to physical well-being. This log can include:

Meals: Tracking what you ate and how you felt afterward might reveal triggers (like dairy leading to bloating or sugar causing energy crashes).

Activity: Logging walks, stretches, or sports.

Mood: Noting stress levels or overall emotional state that day.

Symptoms: Any headaches, stomach issues, or pains that pop up.

Reviewing the journal over time can pinpoint patterns. If a certain food sparks discomfort or a weekly event triggers migraines, you can take steps to avoid or manage it.

Making Health a Shared Venture

Sometimes, tackling health goals with friends or loved ones offers motivation. A Cancer might plan healthy meal nights, group walks, or gentle workout sessions with a buddy. This helps them stick to routines while also enjoying a sense of closeness.

Collaborative Ideas

Meal Prep Meetups: A few friends gather to cook multiple healthy dishes for the week.

Online Workouts: Join a video call where each person does a workout at home, then chat afterward about how it went.

Family Activity Time: If you have kids or relatives living with you, schedule a short evening walk or mild dance session together.

Travel and Health Precautions

If Cancer travels—whether for fun or family visits—health routines might get disrupted. Different foods, time zones, or climates can cause discomfort.

Smart Travel Tips

Pack Some Essentials: Medications you rely on, plus simple first-aid items (like band-aids and mild pain relievers).

Stay Hydrated on Flights: Airplane cabins are dry, so drink enough water.

Avoid Overpacked Schedules: Leave room for rest and sleep. Tiring yourself out while traveling can weaken the immune system.

Try Local Foods Carefully: Ease into unfamiliar cuisine. If uncertain, pick well-cooked meals or known safe spots.

Checking In on Mental Health Regularly

A daily or weekly mental check-in can prevent emotional issues from escalating. This practice goes hand in hand with physical health, as the two are connected.

Questions to Ask

- "What made me feel happy or calm this week?"
- "Which moments triggered stress or worry?"
- "Is there something I can do to ease that stress next time?"
- "Am I being fair to myself, or am I being too harsh?"

Writing answers in a journal or telling a close friend can bring clarity. Recognizing mental changes early leads to quicker solutions.

Herbal Teas and Soothing Brews

Herbal teas like chamomile, mint, or lemon balm might calm the nervous system. While they are not medical cures, they can serve as gentle aids for relaxation. Some people find a warm herbal drink before bed helps them sleep better.

However, it is wise to check for allergies or interactions with medications if you drink certain herbs in large amounts. For instance, some herbs might not mix well with blood thinners or other prescriptions. A quick chat with a pharmacist can ensure safety.

Summary: Nurturing the Body, Mind, and Heart

For Cancer, health is tied to both physical care and emotional well-being. Tension or mood swings can impact digestion, sleep, and energy. By taking mindful steps—like regular checkups, balanced meals, gentle exercise, and emotional management—this sensitive sign can stay strong and resilient.

It helps to remember that self-care is not selfish. Maintaining good health allows Cancer to keep sharing kindness without draining themselves. Whether it is a short walk by the water, a careful approach to meal planning, or a regular talk with supportive friends, these small habits add up. Staying healthy means Cancer can continue to do what they do best: care, protect, and foster warmth in their surroundings.

CHAPTER 18: SUPPORT FOR PERSONAL GOALS

Cancer is known for compassion and family ties, but this does not mean they lack dreams or ambitions of their own. In fact, many Cancers hold deep personal goals—whether related to home life, career, creativity, or community projects. The challenge is that they can sometimes place others' needs before their own, or feel stuck due to shyness or fear of rejection.

This chapter offers practical advice to help Cancers define, pursue, and achieve personal goals. From brainstorming meaningful aims to tackling obstacles like self-doubt or lack of time, we will explore how Cancer's nurturing nature can be harnessed for self-directed success. By taking care of their own dreams, they can become even stronger sources of help to loved ones.

Why Goals Matter for Cancer

Having clear goals can give Cancer a sense of direction and purpose, stopping them from drifting in day-to-day tasks that might lack deeper meaning. Goals also help Cancer maintain a healthy balance between caring for others and focusing on personal development.

When a Cancer invests energy in their dreams—be it writing a short story, training for a new job skill, or saving for a cozy home—they build confidence and show themselves that personal needs deserve attention too. This inner confidence often radiates outward, making them even better supporters for friends and family.

Identifying Core Values

Before setting goals, it helps to clarify what truly matters. Cancer might list values such as family harmony, emotional well-being, creativity, or community service. By linking goals to core values, motivation stays strong.

Values Exploration Exercise

Write down at least five traits or activities that make life feel meaningful (e.g., "family closeness," "helping others," "expressing creativity," "financial security," or "learning new skills").

Think about how these values show up in daily life. Are there tasks or roles that support these values, or do they get pushed aside?

Brainstorm ways to align goals with these values. For instance, if "helping others" is a key value, a career shift to a helping profession might be considered.

Brainstorming Personal Goals

Some people have a clear dream in mind—like starting a small business or writing a book. Others feel uncertain, as they have been so focused on caring for loved ones. Cancer might need to ask, "What would make me feel fulfilled, even if no one else asked for it?"

Goal Brainstorming Tips

Mind Mapping: Grab a paper, draw a circle with "My Goals" in the center, and branch out possible aims: "Health," "Family," "Career," "Art," "Community," "Finance," etc. Write any ideas that arise.

Think Big, Then Refine: List wild ideas without limiting yourself. Later, narrow down to a few that feel exciting and feasible.

Look at Role Models: Notice people you admire—maybe a friend who returned to school, an online creator, or a relative who overcame obstacles. What about their actions inspires you?

Brainstorming freely helps break any mental cage. Later steps will bring realism, but the start should be open.

Sorting Goals by Priority

After listing possible goals, it can help to rank them by how important and time-sensitive they are. Some might be short-term (like learning a new recipe), while others are long-term (saving for a home).

Priority Categories

High Priority: Goals that align closely with values and have pressing timelines (like finishing a degree program, applying for a specific job, or addressing a health need).

Medium Priority: Goals that matter but can be paced more slowly (like improving a hobby or exploring volunteer options).

Low Priority: Good ideas with no urgent timeline, which can be revisited later.

When a Cancer sees all goals in a single list, they can decide where to focus first. This step reduces overwhelm, helping them avoid trying to do everything at once.

Setting SMART Goals

SMART stands for Specific, Measurable, Achievable, Relevant, and Time-bound. Applying this method can guide Cancer toward concrete progress instead of vague wishes.

Specific: For instance, "I want to learn to bake bread once a week" instead of "I want to be a better cook."

Measurable: Aiming to read 10 pages a day or save a certain amount each month.

Achievable: The goal should be realistic given current resources or constraints.

Relevant: Linked to personal values or interests (no point learning guitar if you have zero interest in music).

Time-bound: Having a deadline or timeframe. For example, "By the end of next month," or "Within six months."

Making goals SMART often prevents confusion and fosters a sense of direction.

Overcoming Self-Doubt

Cancers may hold back from ambitious aims, fearing they might fail or let others down. This self-doubt can sabotage progress. Recognizing such thoughts is the first step.

Strategies

Positive Self-Talk: Replace "I'm not talented enough" with "I can learn by practicing or seeking advice."

Small Wins: Tackle smaller steps first to build confidence. If you see small successes, it is easier to believe in bigger ones.

Focus on Growth: Even if you fail a part of the plan, each attempt teaches new skills. A "failure" can be a lesson, not a dead end.

Support Systems: Friends or mentors who encourage you can counteract self-doubt. Ask them for honest feedback and reminders of your strengths.

Balancing Personal Goals with Family Duties

Cancer often puts family at the top of the list, which is loving but can eat up personal time. If you have children, older relatives, or a busy household, you might struggle to find space for your own pursuits.

Ways to Balance

Shared Activities: Can your family join a part of your goal? For instance, if learning to cook healthy meals is your aim, involve children in meal prep. If improving fitness is the goal, go for family walks.

Scheduled "Me Time": Block out a set period—maybe early morning or after dinner—strictly for your personal project. Let family know this is your focus time.

Ask for Help: If possible, have a partner, sibling, or friend watch the kids for an hour so you can work on your art or study. Cancer should remember it is okay to lean on others sometimes.

Finding synergy between personal dreams and family life can make you feel less torn.

Time Management Skills

A sign that cares for many people can feel pulled in multiple directions. Good time management ensures personal goals do not get lost.

Tips

Daily To-Do List: Write tasks each morning or the night before. Highlight the most important ones (both personal and household).

Use a Planner: Whether a paper planner or a phone app, schedule tasks in blocks. Include rest or buffer times so you are not rushed.

Avoid Perfection: If you wait for the perfect moment to start a task, you may never begin. Do the best with the time available.

Say "No" Tactfully: If new requests pop up that do not align with your priorities, politely refuse or postpone them.

With structured time blocks, Cancer can guard moments for personal goals and still be there for loved ones.

Resources and Learning

Often, goals require new knowledge or skills. Cancer might feel uneasy stepping into unfamiliar areas, but learning can be exciting when linked to a heartfelt aim.

Finding Resources

Online Tutorials: Websites with free or paid lessons for almost any skill—cooking, coding, painting, etc.

Local Workshops: Community centers might host short classes in languages, crafts, or business.

Libraries: Books and digital resources can be a goldmine, and librarians can guide you to relevant info.

Mentors: If you know someone skilled in your area of interest, ask for guidance. People often enjoy passing on their expertise.

Creating a Support Network

Besides mentors, having a supportive circle keeps motivation up. Look for friends or group members who cheer each other on rather than criticize.

Support System Ideas

Accountability Partner: Pair up with a friend who also has a goal. Check in weekly, share updates, and encourage each other.

Online Communities: There are forums or social media groups for almost any goal—like healthy eating, writing short stories, or building small businesses.

Family Involvement: If loved ones understand your aims, they can offer help or at least reduce demands during your focus hours.

Make sure to communicate with these folks about what kind of support you need—some might think constructive criticism is helpful, while you might just want upbeat motivation.

Handling Emotional Waves During Goal Pursuit

Cancers experience mood shifts that might interrupt momentum. One day they feel fired up, the next they feel self-critical or anxious. Recognizing this pattern allows for planning.

Mood Management

Plan for Low Days: Have a list of simpler tasks to do when motivation dips (like reading up on ideas or doing easy chores related to the goal).

Visual Reminders: A vision board or pictures can reignite energy if you are feeling down. Maybe post a photo of a dream house or a scene that symbolizes success.

Reward System: Promise yourself a small treat—like a relaxing bath or a favorite snack—after finishing a tricky step.

Mood swings do not have to block progress if you adapt your actions to how you feel on any given day.

Overcoming Fear of Criticism

Cancer can be sensitive to what others think. Fear of negative feedback might stop them from sharing a work-in-progress or applying for a public role. Learning to handle feedback calmly is key to moving forward.

Approach

Seek Safe Feedback First: Show your early draft or idea to a supportive friend who is honest but kind.

Gradual Public Steps: If you are writing a blog, maybe share small parts with a select group before going public.

Self-Validation: Remind yourself that everyone starts somewhere. Criticism can guide improvement if it is constructive. If feedback is simply mean, it may reflect the critic's own issues rather than your worth.

Money and Funding Goals

Some ambitions need funds—like starting a small business, renovating a space, or paying for classes. If finances are tight, a Cancer might feel anxious. A clear plan can reduce money stress.

Money Tips

Budget: List monthly income and expenses, seeing where you can trim non-essentials to save for the goal.

Separate Savings: Open a small separate account for the specific goal. Even small deposits add up.

Look for Grants or Scholarships: Some fields offer financial support for training or projects.

Crowdfunding: If your idea helps the community, consider an online funding platform. Remember to research fees and rules.

Building a cushion can take time. Patience and steady saving build confidence, ensuring you feel stable while chasing the dream.

Celebrating Milestones

As you progress, it is crucial to mark small achievements to stay motivated.

Ways to Mark Achievements

Personal Notes: Write down what you accomplished and how it feels. Keep these notes in a jar or a journal.

Share with Friends: Talk about your progress. Genuine cheer from loved ones can spur you on.

Meaningful Treat: Plan an afternoon off, buy a new book, or enjoy a special meal that signifies a step forward.

Look Back: Compare where you started to where you are now. Reminding yourself of growth can reinforce that your effort matters.

Making Adjustments Along the Way

Goals can evolve. Sometimes, new information arises, or interests shift. Cancer might worry about "giving up," but changing course is not failure if it aligns better with true aspirations.

Adaptation Strategies

Regular Reviews: Every month or so, revisit your goals. Are they still relevant?

Check the Why: If motivation dips, recall why you chose that aim. If the reason no longer holds, it may be time to shift focus.

Healthy Pivot: If you realize you prefer painting over writing, pivoting might be wise. Use what you learned from the old plan as you move to the new direction.

This flexibility keeps the path alive and real, rather than forcing you to continue a path that no longer fits.

Dealing with Setbacks

No plan goes perfectly. A sudden financial challenge, health issue, or family emergency can disrupt progress. Cancers might become discouraged or feel guilty if they cannot maintain the pace.

Handling Setbacks

Pause and Reassess: Maybe reduce the goal's speed but do not abandon it entirely if it still matters to you.

Seek Understanding: Let supportive individuals know you have run into obstacles. They might offer solutions or moral support.

Focus on Small Steps: Instead of halting everything, do what you can. Even a bit of effort can preserve momentum.

These dips are normal in any long-term project. With patience and self-compassion, you can bounce back.

Taming Perfectionism

Cancer might want everything to be just right, especially if they tie personal worth to the success of their endeavors. But perfectionism can lead to procrastination or never feeling satisfied.

Ways to Overcome

Set "Good Enough" Standards: Aim for a solid outcome instead of absolute flawlessness.

Time-Limited Work: If you must write, set a timer for a certain period. Whatever is done in that window is acceptable for the day.

Acceptance of Flaws: Mistakes are part of learning. Each rough patch can guide you to do better next time.

Reward Completion: Finishing a project is an achievement, even if some details could be polished further.

Sharing Success with Loved Ones

When a goal starts showing results—like a finished craft, a published article, or a well-earned qualification—Cancer might feel shy about stepping into the spotlight. But sharing success can foster a sense of pride and let supportive people celebrate with you.

How to Share

Tell a Close Friend or Relative: They might want to hear updates, cheer you on, or help you mark the occasion.

Social Media: A brief post to announce a milestone can bring encouraging responses.

Give Thanks: If others assisted, express gratitude. Feeling gratitude can deepen bonds and affirm their help meant a lot.

While humility is good, letting others know about achievements can bring more support and open new doors.

Turning Passions into Side Projects or Careers

If a Cancer's dream is to turn a hobby into income—like catering, writing, or craft sales—small steps can test viability without risking everything at once.

Starting a Side Venture

Pilot Run: Try selling or showcasing your product or service on a small scale, such as local markets or online platforms, to see how people respond.

Budget for Startup: Keep track of materials or fees. If costs outweigh gains, adjust the approach.

Separate Accounts: Manage project earnings in a different account to see net profit.

Steady Growth: Expanding slowly avoids burnout and big financial risks.

A measured approach can help a nurturing sign avoid undue stress while exploring new professional horizons.

Handling External Pressure and Opinions

Family or peers may have expectations—such as wanting you to follow a certain career path or handle daily tasks instead of pursuing your own aims. Standing firm in your goals, while respecting loved ones, is often tricky for Cancer.

Communication Tips

Explain the Why: Share why the goal matters to you. Emphasize you are not abandoning duties but seeking personal growth.

Suggest a Plan: Show how you will keep up with major responsibilities while dedicating some time to your dream.

Ask for Support: If you need less interference, politely say, "I'd appreciate encouragement more than advice right now."

Hold Boundaries: If someone keeps pushing you in a different direction, calmly restate your stance.

Motivational Reminders for a Sensitive Sign

Cancer might lose drive if they feel discouraged or if emotions shift. Setting up gentle motivators can keep energy flowing.

Affirmation Notes: Write short, supportive phrases on sticky notes—"You can do this!"—and place them where you often look (mirror, desk, or fridge).

Inspirational Reads: Keep a book of short quotes or stories about people who overcame doubts or grew from small starts. Read a bit whenever you feel stuck.

Visual Progress Chart: Hang a simple chart to mark completed tasks. Seeing consistent progress, even small, can spark a sense of achievement.

Community Service as a Goal

Some Cancers feel called to do charitable or helpful work for a local group. Setting a structured goal can keep these efforts focused and purposeful, whether collecting items for donation or organizing a small event.

Planning Service Projects

Research Needs: Learn what your community or chosen cause requires most.

Form a Team: Invite friends or neighbors to help gather items, spread the word, or plan the event.

Set Timelines: Choose a date or short period to see the project through.

Reflect on Impact: After finishing, note what went well and what can improve next time.

This merges Cancer's caring spirit with personal growth, as leading a project builds organizational and social skills.

Travel or Exploration Goals

If a Cancer dreams of seeing new places but feels nervous leaving familiar surroundings, a gradual approach can ease them in.

Short Trips First: Weekend getaways or local tourist spots can build comfort with traveling.

Plan Comfort Items: Bring a favorite blanket or pillow if staying overnight. Familiar touches can soothe travel anxiety.

Research: Learn about the destination's culture and safety tips. Well-prepared journeys reduce stress.

Stay Connected: If leaving family behind is a worry, agree on regular call times.

Exploring new places can broaden horizons, inspire creativity, and reveal fresh personal interests, all while balancing Cancer's need for security.

Tech Tools for Goal Tracking

Apps and websites designed for habit tracking or project management can help keep goals on schedule. Cancer might find it simpler to track progress digitally if they prefer structured steps.

Habit Trackers: Apps that let you mark daily habits, showing streaks and sending gentle reminders.

Project Tools: Trello or Asana for bigger tasks, where you can create boards, to-do lists, and deadlines.

Digital Journals: Online diaries or note apps to jot down thoughts, experiences, and progress snapshots.

Choosing a tool that feels comfortable is key. If an app is too complex, it might add stress rather than help.

Celebrating Achievements

Cancer might not want loud parties, but a calm, meaningful moment can reward consistent work.

Gentle Ways

Write a Thank-You Note to Yourself: Express gratitude for the effort and perseverance you have shown.

Light a Special Candle: Reflect on how far you have come. This can become a personal ritual each time a goal checkpoint is reached.

Invite a Close Friend: Share a cozy meal or a relaxed hangout to talk about your journey.

Such acts remind you that personal goals matter. You deserve recognition for each step of the path.

Handling Guilt About Self-Focus

Cancer might feel guilt if they devote time to personal ambitions instead of always helping family. But personal growth does not mean abandoning loved ones; it can enrich your ability to care for them in the future.

Reframing

Long-Term Benefits: Gaining new skills or financial stability can help support family better over time.

Modeling Self-Care: By valuing your goals, you teach children or siblings that it is healthy to have personal aims, too.

Quality Over Quantity: If you invest in yourself, the time you spend with loved ones may become more joyful and less resentful.

Steps After Reaching a Major Goal

When you reach a big milestone—finishing school, publishing an article, or saving up for a house—there might be a sense of "What's next?" Cancers can slip into a lull if they do not plan for the next stage.

Reflect: Look back on lessons learned during the process. Which strategies worked best for you?

Share Knowledge: You could help someone else who is just starting a similar path, offering insights.

Set New Goals: These can build upon your success or pivot to a different interest. Growth does not have to stop.

You might also choose a restful period to just enjoy the accomplishment. A balanced approach lets you recharge before taking on a new challenge.

Stories of Resilient Cancer Personalities

Though we will discuss notable Cancer figures in the next chapter (Chapter 19), many well-known individuals with Cancer-like traits overcame hurdles to succeed. Hearing about them can be motivating. Some might have balanced family obligations with creative careers, or started community projects despite initial doubts.

In reading their accounts, you might see patterns: the same sensitivity that causes worry can fuel empathy and persistence. A supportive friend or mentor often played a key role. With determination and the right environment, Cancers can accomplish goals that benefit both themselves and those around them.

CHAPTER 19: NOTABLE CANCER FIGURES

Throughout history, many individuals with Cancer-like traits have stood out for their empathy, commitment, and intuition. While not everyone believes in strict astrological patterns, it can still be interesting to see how certain themes appear in the lives of those born under this sign. In this chapter, we will look at a range of notable figures—artists, leaders, philanthropists, and more—who share key Cancer birth dates (approximately June 21 to July 22). We will explore how their personalities, achievements, or life stories might reflect qualities tied to Cancer: caring for others, emotional depth, perseverance, and a wish to create a supportive environment.

This list is only a small sample, as there are countless Cancer figures across the world. Some are well-known celebrities, while others may be less famous but influential in their fields or communities. In highlighting these examples, we hope to show how Cancer strengths can manifest in varied paths, whether through creativity, public service, or quiet dedication to family and society.

Artists and Performers

Many Cancer personalities bring a strong emotional core to their work. Their art might capture deep feelings, personal stories, or a sense of human connection.

Frida Kahlo (born July 6, 1907): A renowned Mexican painter, famous for self-portraits that revealed her pain and resilience. Her art often reflected her physical struggles, personal relationships, and cultural identity. Kahlo's direct portrayal of feelings—whether it was suffering or strength—mirrors Cancer's readiness to engage with emotional reality. She also had a strong sense of home and roots, making her house (the "Blue House" in Mexico City) a notable part of her identity.

Princess Diana (born July 1, 1961): While not an artist in the usual sense, Princess Diana was known for her empathetic public presence. She supported charitable causes related to children, health, and those in need. People often noted her warm demeanor and genuine concern for others. Her personal challenges showed the sensitivity that is sometimes linked to Cancer, and her caring spirit made a lasting impact worldwide.

Sylvester Stallone (born July 6, 1946): An actor, writer, and director, best known for the "Rocky" and "Rambo" franchises. Stallone's "Rocky" character, especially, reflects determination and heart—traits that can resonate with Cancer's perseverance. While the characters he portrays can be tough, there is often an undercurrent of loyalty and emotional drive behind them.

Meryl Streep (born June 22, 1949): Considered one of the greatest film actresses, recognized for her emotional range and ability to portray deeply human roles. Meryl Streep's skill in capturing nuanced feelings has led to numerous honors. Her adaptability and empathy may align with Cancer's intuitive approach, allowing her to inhabit characters with great warmth or complexity.

Leaders and Social Activists

Some Cancers channel their nurturing qualities into leadership or advocacy. They strive to create supportive structures—whether in politics, social justice, or community work.

Nelson Mandela (born July 18, 1918): Though his chart is often associated with a cusp date, many link him to Cancer traits such as compassion, dedication, and a commitment to unity. Mandela's focus on reconciliation and healing in South Africa—after his release from prison—reflects a Cancer-like desire to bring people together, protect the vulnerable, and value emotional bonds within a community.

Malala Yousafzai (born July 12, 1997): A Pakistani activist for female education, and the youngest Nobel Prize laureate. Her bravery and empathy stand out: she risked her safety to speak up for girls' right to attend school. Malala's caring vision for a better future—combined with resilience—can be seen as reflecting Cancer's protective side. She continues to advocate for educational opportunities, showing both emotional depth and a focused goal.

Helen Keller (born June 27, 1880): An American author and activist who overcame the challenges of being deaf and blind. Keller learned to communicate through enormous perseverance, then dedicated her life to improving conditions for others with disabilities. Her sense of empathy and her mission to support those in need show a strong alignment with Cancer's heartfelt approach. Keller's achievements also highlight the determination often associated with this sign.

Writers and Thinkers

Writing can be a powerful medium for Cancers, letting them express emotional insight. These figures used words to share empathy, raise awareness, or delve into human experiences.

Ernest Hemingway (born July 21, 1899): Known for his sparse style, Hemingway wrote classic novels and short stories that often explored courage, conflict, and personal challenge. Although not typically described as "emotional," his characters often faced deep inner struggles—hinting at underlying sensitivity. His personal life included friendships and loyalties that reflected a protective or devoted side, sometimes overshadowed by the public image of machismo.

Paulo Coelho (born August 24, 1947): Although some sources put his birth outside the Cancer range, certain records mention different birth data, so his alignment with Cancer traits is debated. Coelho's famous novel "The Alchemist" speaks of personal quests and following the heart, themes that might attract Cancer readers. Regardless of exact birth data, the emphasis on spiritual and emotional journeys resonates with the sign's introspective nature.

Octavia E. Butler (born June 22, 1947): A pioneering American science fiction writer, recognized for exploring social ideas, empathy, and human nature in her works. She combined imaginative settings with deep character insights, possibly reflecting Cancer's intuition and care for emotional depth. Her protagonists often navigated uncertain worlds, standing strong while displaying vulnerability—a combination that can echo Cancer's protective yet tender side.

Business and Innovation

Cancer's ability to sense people's needs can extend to business or innovation. Some personalities harness empathic understanding to create products or manage teams effectively.

Arianna Huffington (born July 15, 1950): Co-founder of The Huffington Post and founder of Thrive Global, focusing on well-being and work-life balance. Her emphasis on preventing burnout and improving personal resilience could align with Cancer's concern for emotional health and nurturing. She also led significant editorial and entrepreneurial efforts, balancing business sense with a personal, caring brand.

Elon Musk (born June 28, 1971): Known for founding or leading companies like Tesla, SpaceX, and others. Musk's visionary approach might seem more Aquarian or fiery, yet the birth date places him under Cancer. He shows determination, holding onto goals even when odds seem against him. Despite a sometimes direct or controversial public image, there could be an underlayer of personal ideals that resonates with Cancer's desire to protect the future (through sustainable energy or space exploration).

Musicians and Entertainers

Many Cancer-born musicians and entertainers channel strong feelings into performances, reaching fans on an emotional level.

Selena Gomez (born July 22, 1992): A singer and actress who has openly discussed mental health challenges, showing Cancer-like honesty about feelings. Her music often touches on personal themes of heartbreak, recovery, and self-discovery. She also founded cosmetic and philanthropic lines that highlight mental wellness, reflecting care for her audience beyond entertainment.

Ariana Grande (born June 26, 1993): Another pop star known for powerful vocal emotion, weaving personal stories into her songs. She has been involved in charity efforts, such as benefit concerts for victims of tragic events. This mix of artistic passion and caring outreach can match Cancer's empathy and willingness to comfort others.

Lionel Messi (born June 24, 1987): Though a soccer star, not a musician, Messi's athletic style might show traits often associated with Cancer—loyalty to a longtime club (Barcelona for many years), emotional ties to his team, and a humble approach despite vast success. He also supports children's charities. His quiet but impactful presence can exemplify how Cancer can be a strong figure without constant showiness.

Quiet Influencers and Community Figures

Not all influential Cancers are famous worldwide. Many are local community organizers, teachers, or caregivers whose efforts transform neighborhoods or families. They may start youth clubs, run food drives, or mentor young people. These unsung heroes reflect Cancer's protective, giving nature in daily life.

For instance:

A volunteer who organizes after-school programs for kids in a tough neighborhood, offering them a safe space to learn and grow.

A nurse who goes beyond standard duties to comfort patients' families, embodying empathy at the hospital.

A parent who fosters children or sets up charitable events to support them, ensuring each child feels secure and valued.

These local heroes might not be public names, but they demonstrate Cancer's core—lifting others through heartfelt generosity.

Themes in Cancer Stories

When we examine the lives of many Cancer-born individuals, certain patterns may appear (though each person is unique):

Emotional Expression: They often show strong feeling in their art, speeches, or actions, connecting with audiences on a personal level.

Protective Instinct: Many champion causes or defend vulnerable groups, whether through charity, leadership, or activism.

Resilience Through Struggles: Even facing setbacks—physical ailments, social barriers, personal challenges—these figures keep going, motivated by a deep sense of purpose.

Focus on Home or Roots: Some place special emphasis on family ties or cultural identity, weaving it into their public work or creative output.

Of course, these traits can mix with other astrological influences, personal backgrounds, or random life events. Still, the consistent presence of empathy and perseverance suggests a link to Cancer energies.

Lessons from These Figures

While it is fun to identify famous Cancers, the real takeaway is often how they used empathy or emotional depth to shape their paths. Whether through painting, activism, science, or business, they showed that sensitivity can be a strength. Instead of viewing emotion as a drawback, they harnessed it to drive meaningful accomplishments.

Encouragement for Readers

Your caring side can guide you to help others or create heartfelt works.

Struggles in life do not need to stop you; they can add depth to your character and fuel your motivations.

Balancing personal ambition with empathy is possible. Many of these figures found ways to advance their passions while also uplifting people around them.

By seeing these examples, you might feel inspired to lean into your inner warmth, trusting that your intuitive sense and desire for security can lead to real achievements and community impact.

Why These Stories Resonate

Cancer is sometimes labeled as shy or overly sensitive in casual astrology talk, but the figures mentioned here remind us that those traits can spark great things when directed well. Emotional insight can push someone to champion the underprivileged, paint a masterpiece that connects to universal feelings, or build a business that respects customers' needs.

Also, many overcame personal trials—health issues, tough childhoods, or public criticism—yet pressed on. Their experiences highlight that emotional depth can pair with resilience, a mix that fosters compassion for others going through hard times. This synergy of feeling and perseverance can be an asset, not a weakness.

Reflecting on Your Own Potential

If you identify with Cancer, exploring the lives of these individuals might open your mind to new possibilities. You do not have to be a global superstar to put Cancer qualities to use. Even small steps—like local volunteering or learning a new craft—can let you express empathy and care in meaningful ways.

Ideas for Personal Reflection

Which stories or personalities inspire you the most?

What qualities do you admire in them—empathy, courage, or commitment to a cause?

How can you apply a similar approach in your life, on any scale?

These reflections might boost your confidence in following personal dreams or giving back to your community.

Caution: Birthdates and Astrological Accuracy

While we assign people to zodiac signs based on typical birth ranges, real astrological charts also depend on time and place of birth. Sometimes, a day or two near the sign's transition can shift whether someone is a Cancer or a Gemini/Leo. Also, birth data can be disputed or recorded differently across sources.

Hence, seeing these figures as examples is more about noticing possible themes rather than rigid proof of astrological correctness. If you spot a minor difference in a birth date that places them in another sign, it is no big issue. Their stories can still illustrate how empathy, care, and resilience can shape remarkable lives.

Other Cancer Figures and Wider Diversity

There are countless Cancer-born individuals in sports, science, media, government, and more. Some might include:

Jaden Smith (born July 8, 1998): Actor and musician, recognized for philanthropic and environmental efforts.

Robin Williams (born July 21, 1951): Actor and comedian known for comedic genius and heartfelt roles, though some date records list him close to the Leo cusp.

Mike Tyson (born June 30, 1966): Famous boxer with a strong persona, yet also known for vulnerable admissions about personal struggles.

Exploring deeper can reveal Cancers from every culture and domain. The unifying thread often remains an emotional approach, blended with loyalty and the urge to protect or uplift.

How to Find Inspiration in Their Stories

Look for Overcoming Hardship: Many faced barriers—health crises, social prejudice, or personal loss. Notice the ways they handled these issues.

Study Their Support Systems: Did they have a mentor, a family circle, or close friends who helped them succeed? This can remind you to lean on supportive people in your life.

Identify Key Traits: Did they use empathy to connect with an audience or customers? Did they build loyal teams through trust? Did they stay true to personal principles despite challenges?

Connect It to Your Goals: If you dream of a creative career, see how an artist overcame self-doubt. If you want to help a cause, read how an activist found resources and allies.

This process can be a quiet learning curve, letting you adapt their methods or mindsets to your own reality.

Stories from Your Local Area

You might also explore local figures who reflect Cancer values. Perhaps a neighbor launched a neighborhood cleanup program or founded a small nonprofit that supports single parents. Seeking these local examples can be just as motivating as looking at global celebrities. You can even speak with them to hear firsthand how they stayed determined and balanced their own emotional well-being.

Local stories carry the advantage of direct contact or personal relevance. You see how someone in similar conditions or community settings made a difference. This closeness can spark practical ideas.

Passing on the Legacy of Care

One outcome of learning about notable Cancers is realizing how each individual's empathy can ripple through society. When we see Princess Diana's efforts with charities or Malala's push for education, we recognize that a caring heart, combined with action, can shape entire movements. The question becomes: how can we, in our own ways, continue that legacy?

Volunteer More: Even a small commitment—like reading at a nursing home or tutoring at a local center—can reflect that caring spirit.

Mentor Younger People: If you have knowledge in a certain field, guiding someone can pay forward the supportive approach Cancer so often embodies.

Spread Hope: Speak up for those who cannot voice their needs, or comfort someone who feels isolated. Compassionate words can make a large difference.

This cycle of empathy means that each generation of caring folks draws from the example of those who came before, adding their own imprint on the world.

Personal Reflection: Finding Your Unique Path

Not everyone aims for global fame or massive social change, and that is perfectly fine. One of the key lessons from these Cancer icons is that you can use empathy and resilience in any sphere—at home, at work, or in your local environment. Greatness does not always mean a stage or a big audience; it can be quietly transforming lives around you, building small but meaningful successes.

Questions

Which Cancer trait do you feel strongest about—your empathy, your creativity, or your loyalty?

How might you channel it into your daily activities?

Is there a small step you can take right now toward a cause or project that aligns with your caring side?

The Ups and Downs of Fame or Public Life

Looking at celebrities or known leaders also reminds us that a Cancer's sensitivity can be both a strength and a vulnerability. Some faced mental health struggles, criticisms from media, or pressure from fans. Learning about their coping strategies—whether therapy, retreats, or trusted advisors—reinforces that handling emotional intensity is a skill to practice, not a once-and-done fix.

If you ever aim for a bigger platform, consider how you will guard your own well-being. The nurturing approach you extend to others must also apply to yourself.

Future Notable Cancers

The future likely holds many more Cancer-born influencers who will address global issues, break new ground in art or science, or create supportive businesses. Some may be reading this book right now. It is exciting to think about how emerging voices might use technology, social networks, or unconventional ideas to make an impact, guided by empathy and a protective mindset.

Who knows—you might be part of that wave, whether as a quiet community organizer or a public figure. The sign's heritage suggests you have the capacity to inspire, comfort, and unite. You only need to bring your vision forward.

The Balance of Hype vs. Realism

It is easy to get carried away by star sign lists praising "famous Cancers." Yet these individuals are complex humans with a mix of strengths and flaws. Some had personal controversies or dealt with regrets. This honest perspective is key: greatness often arises not from perfection, but from navigating difficulties with sincerity.

By understanding the real ups and downs of their journeys, you see that empathy and loyalty can be steadfast anchors, even when faced with mistakes. That knowledge can boost your own resilience, reminding you that being genuine matters more than being flawless.

CHAPTER 20: FINAL THOUGHTS AND CLOSURE

Over the course of this book, we have explored the Cancer sign in depth. From typical traits and emotional layers to career outlooks, friendships, family ties, creative pursuits, and health tips, we have seen how a person born under Cancer (June 21 to July 22 in many systems) might navigate life. This final chapter aims to bring these themes together, providing a heartfelt conclusion that honors Cancer's distinctive blend of sensitivity, loyalty, and quiet strength.

Whether you identify strongly with every detail or just a few elements ring true, the main lesson is that Cancer's caring nature can be a profound gift. By balancing self-care, personal ambitions, and deep connections with loved ones, those who resonate with Cancer can build a life that feels secure, loving, and meaningful.

Revisiting Key Traits

Emotional Depth: Cancer experiences feelings keenly, which can nurture empathy and close bonds. This emotional side fuels creativity, compassion, and a protective spirit.

Protective Instinct: Like the crab's shell, Cancer's desire to shield loved ones brings comfort to families and communities. Learning to apply this instinct in a healthy way—without smothering or neglecting the self—is crucial.

Intuitive Leanings: Cancer often senses unspoken tensions or joys. This intuition aids in problem-solving, as it offers insights others might miss.

Home and Family Focus: The sign is drawn to secure, warm environments. "Home" can mean a literal house or a sense of belonging with friends, partners, or a chosen community.

Resilience: Under that gentle surface lies considerable determination. Cancer can endure hardships and keep going, especially if motivated by care for others or a cherished goal.

Embracing the Strength of Vulnerability

In a world that sometimes prizes boldness, Cancer's softer approach might seem out of place. Yet vulnerability can be a power. By admitting feelings or uncertainties, Cancer creates authentic ties with others. This openness often inspires trust and loyalty. The key is maintaining boundaries, so sharing does not become oversharing or lead to emotional overload.

Being vulnerable also means acknowledging your own emotional waves. When sadness hits, it is healthier to address it than to bury it. This honest stance helps you navigate mood changes while growing in self-awareness.

Balancing Personal Needs and Care for Others

A recurring challenge for Cancer is striking equilibrium between looking after personal aims and supporting loved ones. If you always prioritize someone else's crisis, your own goals can stall. Conversely, if you focus solely on personal pursuits, you might feel guilt for ignoring your nurturing side.

Healthy tips:

Set Time Slots: Dedicate certain hours for your work or hobbies, and other times for family or friends.

Ask for Help: If you feel pulled in too many directions, request assistance from a partner or friend.

Say "Yes" Wisely: Not every favor must fall on your shoulders. Evaluate your capacity before committing.

When you take care of yourself, you are better able to help the people you love.

Continuing Self-Discovery

The zodiac can be a doorway to introspection, not a final rulebook. You might relate to Cancer's themes but also to traits from your rising sign or your Moon sign. Each chart is unique, shaped by personal history and free will. This book's exploration of Cancer is meant to spark ideas about your emotional style, life rhythms, and potential paths.

Ideas for Growth:

Reflect Often: Journal about feelings, changes in mood, and what triggers them. Learn to see patterns that help or hinder well-being.

Study Other Influences: If astrology intrigues you, look into the positions of your Moon or other planets to gain further insights into your personality.

Stay Open: Life events, new friendships, or career changes can shift how you express Cancer traits. Adaptation is part of personal evolution.

Building a Comfortable Home Base

For many who resonate with Cancer, the home is central. Making a space that feels cozy and safe can ground you emotionally. This does not require a large budget. Even small touches—soft lighting, soothing scents, tidied corners—can foster calm.

Your home can also reflect your interests. Display items that remind you of achievements or cherished memories. If you live with family or roommates, communicate how the shared environment can nourish everyone's sense of belonging. Each person might personalize a corner or bring elements that add warmth.

Communication as a Path to Deeper Bonds

One of Cancer's best gifts is the ability to listen empathetically. Yet sometimes you might hold back from speaking about your own needs, fearing conflict or burdening others. Practicing open dialogue lets you share emotional truths without resentment building.

Communication Pointers:

Use "I Feel" Statements: Instead of blaming, say, "I feel upset when..." so the focus is on your feelings, not on accusing the other person.

Ask for Clarity: If you sense tension, gently inquire, "Is something bothering you?" This direct approach can prevent misunderstandings.

Nonverbal Sensitivity: Since you pick up on subtle cues, confirm them verbally. "I notice you seem quiet. Are you okay?" This blend of intuition and clear words fosters mutual understanding.

Forgiving Yourself for Imperfections

Because Cancer can be self-critical—especially about perceived failures in caring for others or in personal goals—it is important to practice self-forgiveness. Mistakes happen, and no one can be everything to everyone at all times. Recognize that your kind heart is genuine, even if certain tasks or relationships do not turn out perfectly.

When you make an error, see it as a chance to learn. Apologize if needed, fix what you can, and then move on. Dwelling on guilt or shame depletes your emotional reserves, hindering your ability to function at your best. A balanced perspective will keep your spirit intact for the next challenge.

Expanding Relationships Beyond the Shell

Like the crab that might hide away, a Cancer can feel tempted to remain in familiar settings. While comfort is valuable, stepping outside your shell from time to time can lead to new friendships, adventures, or professional opportunities.

Try Light Networking: Even if large social events are daunting, small gatherings or online communities can help you discover allies or mentors.

Share Your Talents: If you paint, sing, or have a hobby, show it to supportive peers. This can open doors for collaboration or feedback.

Volunteer in a New Setting: A local group or cause might expand your circle and let you practice empathy in a fresh context.

Each small step outward can balance Cancer's inward focus, keeping life dynamic rather than static.

Balancing Head and Heart in Decisions

Cancer's emotional instincts are powerful, but big decisions also need logical thought. Whether picking a job, moving to a new city, or starting a family, weigh practical factors alongside gut feelings. Too much reliance on emotion can lead to rushed moves; ignoring feelings altogether might cause regrets.

Approach:

List Pros and Cons: Write them down, noticing how each item makes you feel.

Seek Advice: A grounded friend or expert can see angles you might overlook.

Trust Your Inner Alarm: If something feels deeply off, investigate why. Sometimes intuition is correct in highlighting potential problems.

The Ongoing Need for Self-Care

As emphasized in earlier chapters, self-care underpins a healthy Cancer life. Regular checkups, balanced meals, gentle movement, and emotional outlets keep stress at bay. If you sense yourself slipping—stomachaches, constant fatigue, or overwhelming worry—pause and re-center.

Mini Self-Care Check

- Are you sleeping enough?

- Have you taken a break from screens or stressful news?

- When was the last time you spent quiet time alone or in nature?

- Do you need to speak to someone about your worries?

Listening to these questions daily or weekly can prevent burnout.

Celebrating Wins in Quiet, Meaningful Ways

For a Cancer, big public festivities might feel overwhelming or inauthentic. Finding smaller, meaningful gestures can keep your spirit bright.

Possible ideas:

- Write a reflective letter to yourself about your progress.

- Treat yourself to a home spa night—candles, a soothing bath, and gentle music.

- Invite one or two close friends for a calm meal where you share good news or appreciate each other's support.

Such moments keep you motivated, reminding you that progress, however modest, deserves acknowledgment.

Growing Through Emotional Insights

Over these chapters, we have repeatedly noted Cancer's strong emotional side. Emotions do not have to be random waves; they can be signals telling you about needs, boundaries, or directions. By tuning in, you learn what fosters happiness or triggers sadness.

Active Emotional Learning

- Use journaling or private audio recordings to track emotional patterns.

- If anger arises often, examine underlying frustrations—are you taking on tasks you resent?

- If sadness lingers, consider whether you are missing meaningful connections or spiritual nourishment.

Turning emotions into guides encourages consistent personal evolution.

Being Open to New Phases in Life

Just as the Moon cycles, your life will also shift—starting families, changing careers, losing loved ones, or relocating. Adapting can be tricky for a sign that values security. Yet these transitions can reveal untapped strengths. Your empathy might broaden to new communities, or your creativity might flourish in a different environment.

Staying open means trusting your core—your loyal heart, your caring instincts—no matter the external changes. This helps you feel stable within, even if the outside world rearranges itself.

Inspiring Others

The same compassion you show to friends and family can ripple out to inspire them. By handling personal struggles with honesty, by building a supportive home life, or by standing up for someone in need, you model the power of empathy. Colleagues or younger relatives might look to you for moral support or guidance.

This influence does not require a spotlight. Quiet kindness can shift someone's day or even their outlook on life. In a way, each Cancer has the chance to be a caretaker or mentor, leaving small but profound marks on the people around them.

Leaving a Lasting Legacy

We often think of legacy in terms of large achievements—huge charities, famous works, or public honors. But legacies can also be intimate: the loving environment you create at home, the thoughtful lessons you teach children, the friendships you nurture. These echoes live on in memories, shaping how others approach their own relationships and goals.

Your devotion to home, family, or community can spark a generational ripple effect. When you pass on traditions of warmth and understanding, they become part of collective memory, ensuring that the "Cancer spirit" continues in future families and communities.

Acknowledging the Real Challenges

While focusing on positives, we should not ignore that Cancer can face genuine hurdles:

- Insecurity leading to clinging behavior or fear of rejection.

- Mood swings that cause confusion or strain in relationships.

- Overprotectiveness that limits loved ones' independence.

Recognizing these pitfalls allows for proactive steps: setting healthy boundaries, talking with a counselor if needed, and practicing self-awareness. Each challenge can be managed by mindful habits and genuine effort toward growth.

Summarizing the Chapters

To briefly recap what we have covered in this book:

Introduction and Traits: The essence of Cancer—a water sign with emotional depth, symbolized by a crab's shell.

Emotional Landscape: How feelings shape day-to-day life, relationships, and personal identity.

Home and Family: The protective, cozy side of Cancer, focusing on domestic harmony.

Friendship, Love, and Career: Exploring how Cancer expresses care in personal bonds and job settings, and the need for balance.

Creativity, Self-Care, and Spiritual Dimensions: Ways that Cancer's sensitivity can blossom into art, ritual, or community support, plus the importance of health and personal routines.

Bonds with Other Zodiac Signs: Potential compatibility and friction points, plus how empathy can bridge differences.

Myths, Legends, and Notable Figures: Cultural stories about crabs and references to real-life Cancers who achieved significant results through empathy and persistence.

This final portion underscores how each part interconnects. Mastering emotional equilibrium might ease relationships, which in turn influences career choices or daily well-being.

Moving Forward with Confidence

As you finish this book, consider which sections resonated most. Maybe you found new routines for handling stress, new motivation to chase personal goals, or new clarity about your heartfelt approach to family. Every Cancer's path is different, but the guiding principles—empathy, loyalty, resilience—can be shaped into your personal compass.

Questions to Reflect On:

What is one habit or viewpoint from these chapters that you want to adopt immediately?

Which part of your life could benefit most from the nurturing qualities you have (or plan to develop)?

How can you maintain a healthy emotional balance while aiming for personal dreams?

Keeping these questions in mind can anchor your next steps.

Encouragement for the Future

No sign is perfect, and no single approach works for everyone. Yet Cancer's capacity to empathize, adapt, and protect can be a major asset. You can use these strengths to foster positive change in your circles, whether large or small. Each kind word, supportive action, or creative act adds warmth to the world, and Cancer is well-suited to lead with kindness.

Additionally, continuing your self-growth helps you avoid the traps of worry or over-caring. By setting clear boundaries and nurturing your own heart, you ensure you have the energy to keep giving. Remember, a balanced shell is not just for others—it is for you too.

Concluding Reflections

The Cancer sign represents a bridge between emotion and action, between the personal shell and shared relationships. You have within you a gift for warmth, an ability to form close bonds, and a willingness to stand firm for those you love. Whether you use these traits in a quiet home environment or on a broader social platform, the outcome can be uplifting.

We have covered a wide range of topics—traits, daily habits, health, relationships, career, spirituality, culture, famous examples, and more. The hope is that you feel seen and informed, discovering that caring deeply does not hinder success but can be the very spark that leads to meaningful achievements. If there is one message to carry forward, it is that compassion and self-awareness can coexist with strength and ambition. With the right balance, Cancer can flourish, bringing light and comfort to the world.

Thank you for reading and for embracing the unique qualities that define Cancer. May your path ahead be guided by empathy, resilience, and secure emotional grounding—hallmarks of a sign that values both the tenderness of the heart and the power of steadfast determination.

Help Us Share Your Thoughts!

Dear reader,

Thank you for spending your time with this book. We hope it brought you enjoyment and a few new ideas to think about. If there was anything that didn't work for you, or if you have suggestions on how we can improve, please let us know at **kontakt@skriuwer.com**. Your feedback means a lot to us and helps us make our books even better.

If you enjoyed this book, we would be very grateful if you left a review on the site where you purchased it. Your review not only helps other readers find our books, but also encourages us to keep creating more stories and materials that you'll love.

By choosing Skriuwer, you're also supporting **Frisian**—a minority language mainly spoken in the northern Netherlands. Although **Frisian** has a rich history, the number of speakers is shrinking, and it's at risk of dying out. Your purchase helps fund resources to preserve and promote this language, such as educational programs and learning tools. If you'd like to learn more about Frisian or even start learning it yourself, please visit **www.learnfrisian.com**.

Thank you for being part of our community. We look forward to sharing more books with you in the future.

Warm regards,
The Skriuwer Team

www.ingramcontent.com/pod-product-compliance
Lightning Source LLC
LaVergne TN
LVHW012035070526
838202LV00056B/5504